Naturally Miraculous

Naturally Miraculous

The Way of God as All

PETER STILLA

WIPF & STOCK · Eugene, Oregon

NATURALLY MIRACULOUS
The Way of God as All

Wipf & Stock
An Imprint of Wipf and Stock Publishers
199 W. 8th Ave., Suite 3
Eugene, OR 97401

www.wipfandstock.com

PAPERBACK ISBN: 978-1-6667-8589-0
HARDCOVER ISBN: 978-1-6667-8590-6
EBOOK ISBN: 978-1-6667-8591-3

11/20/23

To my loving family—my wife, Shannon, and my daughters, Sophia and Parrish—for supporting and being with me in spirit, even when their husband and father was often not with them while working on this book, it is dedicated.

Contents

Permissions

Common English Bible (CEB)

Scripture quotations marked (CEB) are taken from the Common English Bible®, CEB® Copyright © 2010, 2011 by Common English Bible.™ Used by permission. All rights reserved worldwide. The "CEB" and "Common English Bible" trademarks are registered in the United States Patent and Trademark Office by Common English Bible. Use of either trademark requires the permission of Common English Bible.

English Standard Version (ESV)

Scripture quotations marked (ESV) are from the ESV® Bible (The Holy Bible, English Standard Version®), © 2001 by Crossway, a publishing ministry of Good News Publishers. Used by permission. All rights reserved. The ESV text may not be quoted in any publication made available to the public by a Creative Commons license. The ESV may not be translated in whole or in part into any other language.

Holman Christian Standard Bible (HCSB)

Scripture quotations marked (HCSB) are taken from the Holman Christian Standard Bible®, Copyright © 1999, 2000, 2002, 2003, 2009 by Holman Bible Publishers. Used by permission. Holman Christian Standard Bible®, Holman CSB®, and HCSB® are federally registered trademarks of Holman Bible Publishers.

King James Version

Scripture quotations marked (KJV) are from The Authorized (King James) Version. Rights in the Authorized Version in the United Kingdom

Preface

THIS WORK WAS INSPIRED by a lifelong interest in religion, theology, and all things spiritual. I have certainly learned a lot over time and acquired a few academic and ecclesiastical bona fides along the way, including a divinity school degree and ministerial ordination. On the other hand, I am not a psychologist, neurologist, or anthropologist, even if some of what you see here may seem to delve into those areas of study. So, you are invited to consider whatever these factors lend to what you are about to read.

I am also of the Christian Universalist faith and a CU minister, and I want to acknowledge that I come to this subject matter from that tradition and perspective. What I hope readers notice is that the CU perspective is fundamentally different from that of other branches of Christianity. Because we are anti-sectarian, we are free to follow the path of truth and wisdom wherever it leads, and if it takes us to other spiritual traditions, especially the Eastern wisdom religions, that's okay too. There is no orthodoxy that needs to be protected, nor should other faiths be considered as opposition. There should be no limits or restrictions on the search for ultimate truth, and it is my own exploration into the heart of Christianity that led me to that conclusion.

Introduction

How Did We Get Here?

THE PREMISE WE'LL BEGIN with seems basic enough, and it is that the spiritual yearnings and expressions of humanity have, throughout our history, gone in the only two directions they could go. The people that constitute what will be called Group One have always sought to discover if they have a connection with the Source of All Being within their own beings. For these people there has been the conviction that whatever it was that created all they could see in the world before them was also responsible for the life within them that allowed for that personal experience. Stands to reason, right? Surely the thinking has been whatever it is that "I am" must be a part of the same creation that accounts for the oceans, mountains, and whatever those tiny lights in the nighttime sky are. So, these first seekers were led inward. They strived to see if they could find in themselves what attribute they possessed that gave them and accounted for the life they were experiencing, and if they could find in it any traces of the Creator that put it there.

We can be sure that this quest began when humanity first evolved into self-awareness and perhaps even before language developed, as hard as that is to fathom. So, while words like "soul" or "spirit" weren't in anyone's vocabulary, that was the direction their wonderment was taking them. This concept of soul has always been a part of human consciousness and is very likely instinctive to us. We are born with this concept embedded in our psychological makeup and have been since we first began walking this planet of ours.

Yet however this concept was arrived at, whether it was instinctive or reasoned, it put humanity on the right track. The inner spiritual pursuit, in which the aspirant withdraws from their sensory experience and focuses intensely on what they conceive is their inner essence or what they truly are, is a genuine path to mystical experience, spiritual realization, Christ consciousness, enlightenment, or whatever one wishes to call it. Eventually, as philosophers and great thinkers from every culture and religion considered this metaphysical reality, what came to be known as the perennial philosophy was formed. This philosophy states that the mystical experience is the common basis of every religion and the divinely sanctioned purpose of human existence. We truly exist only to discover our essential oneness with God. In this philosophy, mysticism is seen as the natural, universal religion; natural in how we are all born with the potential for attaining this experience ingrained in our consciousness, and universal in how it transcends every social, religious, and cultural divider humanity has and unites us all as God's children.

People belonging to Group Two can be characterized in this way. They are those who have the same cosmic questions about human existence common to our species, but for some reason, their search for answers didn't take them on the interior pathway or search for soul as it has for Group One. For these people, the quest for understanding their existence led them to project outwardly, at and even beyond the physical universe they could see. The God they conceived of couldn't be ascertained in their physical environment or by inward examination of their personal selves, so their understanding of Divinity and the meaning of life could only be formulated in the imagination. Stories needed to be created out of whole cloth that could be accepted as truthful, and then taught that way to their social or tribal group. Most significantly, the people of Group Two are those whose spiritual lives necessitated they receive a revelation. They had to have someone who they were led to believe had a direct encounter with God communicate to them how God wanted them to live their lives and what their ultimate destiny was. This message also had to include a rationale for understanding that their lives, or whatever spiritual essence they had that gave them life, continued in some way and was not extinguished at death.

The historical record goes back millennia in describing religious rites and ceremonies Group Two types engaged in, but the characteristic they all share is that they were based on myths and narratives orally passed down for generations. Different civilizations in different parts of the world had different stories to share, but what constituted religious life in each was the belief that however the myths answered the ultimate questions of creation and human existence, those answers could be accepted as objectively true. These myths were accompanied by rules supposedly originating from the supernatural creative forces that needed to be obeyed. These rules helped govern the moral behavior of adherents of the faith and mandated appropriate ways to worship the deity or deities in charge.

Eventually in some of these cultures the revelation they had been seeking finally came to them. A prophet or messianic figure appeared at a certain time and place and convinced the people they were communicating a message from God on how to live divinely sanctioned lives. The religions of Judaism, Christianity, and Islam developed this way, following the arrival of Moses, Jesus, and Mohammed in their respective cultures.

Fast forwarding several millennia to the twenty-first century, Groups One and Two still account for the entirety of humanity's spiritual quest. Group One religious life can be characterized as being based on wisdom, practice, and experience, while that of Group Two is grounded in faith, narrative, and obedience. Due largely to the ascendance of science during this time, there is certainly a far greater percentage of people content to be religious or spiritual nonparticipants than there were over the preceding centuries. For these people science has supposedly answered many of the ultimate questions that were once solely in the religious or metaphysical domain. There also isn't the theocratic coercion and cultural mandates there were over most of recorded history. But while there has been some mixing and appropriation in faith practices and organized religion over time, Groups One and Two have remained mostly intact and mutually exclusive.

We have also seen the religions and spiritual traditions that have emerged to create the historical and institutional frameworks for both our spiritual types. As mentioned, it is the revelation-based, Abrahamic religions of Judaism, Christianity, and Islam to which almost all of Group Two belongs, and it is the Eastern wisdom traditions of Hinduism and Buddhism which account for most Group One spirituality. Over time these religions have evolved and developed elements of both types of faith and practice in them. The Abrahamic religions all have rich histories of mysticism and spiritual realization, while the wisdom traditions have faith elements that provide guidance on cosmology and morality.

But unfortunately, the way in which the largest of the Abrahamic religions is taught and practiced has been profoundly flawed for almost all its history. Christianity is a revelation-based religion that arose to pass on the life story of Jesus and the lessons he taught his followers two millennia ago. However, many of us believe it was meant to be more conducive to Group One spirituality like the Eastern wisdom traditions, and indeed it was much like that the first few centuries after Jesus lived. But the Universalist, strongly mystical religion it was originally was crushed by the arrival of Roman Catholicism. The faith based on Jesus's primary mission, to lead his followers to the kingdom of God and the path of mystical realization, was mostly eradicated so that a Christianity based on adherence to a culturally developed faith narrative and submission to an institutional church could be established. The exclusionary, sectarian church that resulted no longer served the truth or its followers as much as it served itself.

Christianity has taught that above all, followers must earn their way to postmortem paradise by doing and believing everything their church tells them to do and believe. Religious duties are satisfied by obeying certain rules that govern personal behavior and interactions with others, as well as believing the right things about God and the church's articles of faith. Those who successfully do that over their lifetime get the grand prize, eternal life in heaven. Christians usually accept that they have immortal souls, but often there is no thought that they must be cultivated or realized in any meaningful way. The central principle that is followed regarding care of the soul is in keeping them unsullied by sin as much as possible, with sin most often defined as not professing their church's articles of faith or violating its moral or behavioral code. Other than that, they feel they have no obligation, or often even think it's possible, to have a direct and transformative experience of God either in their souls or in the world.

This, of course, has been the typical experience of Christians for centuries, and it is so entrenched it will likely be how most of them experience their religion for a long time to come. But if there is to be a twenty-first century reformation, if Christians are ever to be led on a path of authentic spiritual development and well-being, there must be another option. A return to what Christianity originally was before Roman Catholicism is desperately needed. In this church it will be the mystical Christ that is aspired to, and Jesus is not worshiped but followed, as he asked of us. It is the quest for Christ consciousness that was at the heart of his teachings, and Christians would be served as Jesus desired if the mystical experience/ Christ consciousness was placed as the primary objective of a new way of Christian faith. The goal is that by the end of this work a vision for what such a faith may be like will be presented. But we'll start by saying (spoiler alert) that Christian Universalism would provide an ideal foundation in which this new way of faith can take root.

Before getting there though, a lot of spiritual and theological ground must be covered. We'll examine mysticism from several levels, including the metaphysical principles that play a role in it and the psychological factors that impact it. But the first thing we'll consider is the theological principle of creation known as panentheism.

Chapter 1

Panentheism
Naturally Miraculous Reality

Group One spirituality was kindly portrayed in our introduction, but it would be wrong to think it is always perfectly practiced. Sometimes, those who practice this spirituality view nature and the physical world in a negative light. Many seem to believe that any cognition or data they receive through their senses is only a distraction or barrier to spiritual realization. If there is a belief that nature is without divine substance, it follows that contemplating or comprehending it in any way detracts from the spiritual quest. The enlightened consciousness being sought can only be experienced away from the world in a sensory way, not in it. Contemplating the presence of God in the physical world is not considered important.

Spiritual seekers of all kinds, according to the first theological principle we'll consider, need to broaden their perspective on what constitutes creation/nature/reality. There should be an understanding that Divinity is not only the Source of All Being, but also its substance. God consists of and transcends physical reality as we know it, and also constitutes our essential identities or being. Or, as mystics across the centuries have simply and beautifully described it, all is in God and God is in all. Let's look at how this concept has been formulated over the years into the creation principle known as panentheism.

The first thing to know is that the theological and philosophical concept of panentheism is nothing new, even if the word describing it didn't come into usage until the early nineteenth century.[1] This was when it was introduced as a term to differentiate it from pantheism, which means the belief that God and the universe are identical. But the origin of the belief that God is both the Source and Substance of All Being, meaning God shares in our souls and also constitutes and transcends all of creation, likely goes back to prehistory.

Of course, the same can be said of every concept that seeks to answer the cosmic questions of existence, and if you think about it further, there are only a few ways that pre-scientific humanity could answer those questions. We can assume that back in the day it could have been only an exceedingly tiny percentage of us that held materialistic, purely physical ideations of nature and reality. Heck, it's not that easy today, even with all our scientific know-how, so we can conclude that in prehistory it was virtually impossible.

So, if it can be said that basic human consciousness, especially that of untold thousands of years ago, predisposes us towards theism, it should also be said that our deity only had so many conceivable (by us humans) ways in which to implement creation. Two, according to my extensive study. *Creato ex nihilo*, which most folks are familiar with, is Latin for "creation out of nothing,"[2] and is likely the majority assumption of people today, especially in the Abrahamic faiths. However, the other option is the one we like better. It is the creation theory or principle of panentheism known as emanationism.

Emanationism is the assertion that all the matter comprising the physical universe has never not existed and is in fact an essence of the being of God.[3] In other words, God has never existed as spirit alone because the material component is an essential aspect of what God is. Now this physical aspect hasn't always existed as the planets, stars, galaxies, dark matter, and Lord knows what else comprises the universe at this time. Prior to the big bang of thirteen to fourteenish billion years ago, God's material aspect co-existed with the spiritual aspect in some unimaginable way. But then God *emanated* it to *become* the ridiculously large universe we see a minute part of today, meaning it is divinely imbued in its entirety. Most panentheists are not shy about referring to the universe as God's body, if that helps illustrate the idea. However, the physical and the spiritual are not two separate

---

1. "Panentheism."

2. Griffin, *Reenchantment*, 137.

3. "Emanationism."

aspects of the divine identity. We exist within one unitive divine reality. Not only that, but because the universe is constantly changing and evolving that means God is too. A bit later we'll peek at how this concept is also a fundamental part of what's called process philosophy or theology, which in turn has done a lot to substantiate panentheism in modern thought.

Now granted that was a brainful, but before we move on, let's consider something. Is there anything about emanationism that makes it a heavier lift of logic than *creato ex nihilo*? In other words, and at the risk of over-simplification, is one of these concepts any less believable or conceivable than the other? *Creato ex nihilo* has more history behind it and has become almost an article of faith for many people, but taken strictly on their merits, there is no logical reason to assume a more realistic likelihood for either one. Also, as we'll elaborate on later, history's great mystics and sages have from their elevated levels of consciousness given great credence to the panentheistic nature of reality.

In Scripture and Doctrine

When people who have a strong commitment to religion and spirituality encounter an unfamiliar theological or philosophical concept, they often want to know if or where that concept has been expressed in the religion or faith tradition they belong to. So, we will now look at where panentheism has appeared or been referred to in the Bible, and more importantly, how it's been interpreted in church theology and if it is compatible with prevailing doctrine.

It may be a surprise for many people to hear that in the Bible and Christian doctrinal history, panentheism is virtually ubiquitous. In fact, if every mention of the Christ or presence of God in the Bible were closely examined, it is described as existing everywhere and in everything far more often than not. It is unfortunate that so many Christians today think that the universe somehow operates mindlessly, automatically, and autonomously, without any divine or intelligent influence. It's as if God set the universe in motion at creation and then ran off into the beyond for the past fourteen billion years doing, well, not much of anything.

So why is that? The scientific revolution is mostly responsible, because over the last few centuries science has very effectively depicted the universe as a soulless, automatically running machine. But another major factor in the Christian world is that the church has taught that the Christ has only manifested once in history in the person of Jesus, despite the biblical testimony that suggests otherwise. This can be seen in how the being of Christ within the Trinity has often been mischaracterized as somehow existing separately from Creator God and omnipresent Spirit God while incarnated in the person of Jesus, or that the Christ didn't exist at all before Jesus. A full realization of the biblical Christ and Trinitarian doctrine requires understanding that the three persons of the Trinity truly exist as one God and one Being, and the Christ of the Trinity manifested originally as creation itself. Trinitarianism fully realized means understanding it as synonymous with panentheism. The Father/Creator maintains transcendence over the emanated and incarnated Christ of Creation, and the Holy Spirit permeates all of it and binds it together as One.

In a sense none of this should seem that new to Christians. I certainly recall all the way back to my Sunday school lessons as a child learning that "God is everywhere" and God is in everything, and there is "no spot where God is not." This concept was expressed perfectly by Paul in Eph 4:6: "[There is] one God and Father of all, who is above all and through all and in all" (HCSB). This was meant to convey that God is never separate from creation in any way or anywhere. Eventually, though, a disconnect developed for many of us in our faith development, and it occurred partly through how we came to understand the story of Jesus. The Jesus we learned about didn't come to an already Christ imbued world of Spirit-filled people. It may have been that way originally, but Jesus came to a fallen world of fallen people, and it was his mission to rectify that problem. As the one divinely imbued and begotten offspring of the Creator, he was tasked with giving humanity and creation the opportunity to reconcile itself by aligning with him, God's appointed savior.

So, it is easy to see how this interpretation of the Jesus narrative would have countered the Trinitarian understanding of Christian faith, but if we pull back the lens a bit and take a more wholistic overview of the New Testament, we'll see Trinitarianism/panentheism reestablish itself as the faith's foundational principle. And where this starts to be more evident is in the Gospel of John and Paul's Epistles.

When most people consider where the story of creation is told in the Bible, they think of the book of Genesis at the beginning of the Hebrew Bible. But what often goes unnoticed is that the Christian Bible has its own creation story, seen at the beginning of the Gospel of John.

"In the beginning was the Word, and the Word was with God, and the Word was God. He was in the beginning with God. All things came into being through him, and apart from Him not one thing came into being. What has come into being in him was life, and the life was the light of all people" (John 1:1–4 NRSV). A couple of things about this passage should be understood before trying to interpret it. First, note how it starts with "In the beginning," just as the book of Genesis does. Next, see how what came into being "in him" was life, and "the life was the light of all people." Do you recall in Genesis how God's first command in the act of creation was "Let there be light" (Gen 1:3 NRSV)? Perhaps you may also recall when the Christ was incarnated in human form as Jesus the many times he was described as the light of the world. Finally, don't get too thrown off by the term "Word" in this passage. As the Bible was translated, "Word" was put in place of the original Greek "Logos," which was understood as the template through which creation came into being, later described by the word "Christ."[4]

Using Scripture to assert doctrine or theology can sometimes be misleading, but in this instance, it is so instructive it needed to be included, especially because it is the most substantive description of creation in the Christian Bible. There are numerous verses that describe Christ as not only existing "from the beginning" but also being that which the universe itself consists of. A personal favorite is Col 3:11: "There is only Christ. He is everything and he is in everything,"[5] one of many that can be seen in the Pauline Epistles under closer review.

Putting the scriptural evidence aside for the moment, the most important thing to take from this is that understanding the Christ this way restores how the church has always taught how we are to conceive of the Trinity. The Father/Creator God emanated the Son/Christ creation, and it is all immersed with the Holy Spirit, which binds it together as one God, one divine reality. There are theological implications of this though, and one is that this means there have been two incarnations of Christ, the first being that of creation and second being in the person of Jesus billions of years later. But while some may wonder if that makes Jesus less significant to Christian faith, the view from here is quite the opposite. Thinking of Jesus as imbued with all the glory, greatness, and, yes, divinity of creation magnifies him, not lessens him in any way. Jesus was the indispensable

4. Rohr, *Universal*, 13.

5. Rohr, *Universal*, 16.

exemplar and archetype for humanity and showed us how we are all to be perfected through Christ as he was.

There are other, very big picture implications of this as well. One is that Christianity can be seen as existing eternally and not just for two millennia. Clearly, if the Christ that divinized Jesus has existed from the beginning of time as creation, then what we have worshiped in Jesus over the last second of cosmological time has been a constant presence of the Divine throughout history. God has been loving and guiding humans for millions of years as we've evolved to what we are today. Also, as we understand the Trinity as representative of reality and that it is also a Oneness, we can conceive of the All as somehow One as well. All the distinctions in the universe that humans have made, such as the spiritual and physical, human and divine, creative and created, natural and supernatural, can now be seen as ill-conceived or misunderstood.

The natural-supernatural distinction is of particular interest because it has been explored in great depth in the modern school of thought known as process philosophy. It is well beyond the scope of this book to include an in-depth analysis of process philosophy, and one reason is doing so would require someone who is well above my pay grade. The foundational book of this philosophy, *Process and Reality,* was written by Alfred North Whitehead and published in 1929, and let me tell you, this Whitehead guy was a real smarty-pants. I tried to read it when I was in seminary and my brain locked up on about page two. I felt like an idiot but was later consoled by a professor of mine at Harvard Divinity, Dr. Philip Clayton, who told me there were probably just a few dozen people at that time who fully comprehended it. I did a bit better when I read the process philosophers who came after Whitehead, who were able to explain the philosophy in a way that mere mortals could grasp it. So, this is probably a good a time as any to thank David Ray Griffin, author of 2001's *Reenchantment without Supernaturalism,* for coming to my rescue on this topic.

Whitehead's philosophy was intended in part to show that the gap in how science and religion conveyed reality to the world was not real, because assumptions both sides made on what constitutes the physical and spiritual were based on faulty logic. Process thought made the case that the principles of logic that science used to substantiate materialism really, when fully analyzed, had more of an undermining effect. It shows how science comes with its own set of biases that detract from the supposedly logical foundation of its conclusions and has in many ways failed to meet the epistemological standards it has set for itself.[6]

Cutting to the chase, Whitehead asserted that nothing is permanent or unchanging but is constantly in the process of becoming, and what we have subsequently discovered is that at the atomic level he was right.[7] Even the desk, door, or rock you are looking at now is processing in some way. It may not be apparent for millions of years, but change is constant in everything.

Perhaps as a part of this atomic-level activity constantly taking place in every seemingly static object, process philosophy has also theorized that interior experience is intrinsic to and exists throughout the universe. This concept has come to be known as panpsychism, meaning the universe and all that is in it is pervaded by consciousness of some sort.[8] Whitehead was an early proponent of the idea that no matter how the physical processes of evolution produced brains of greater and greater complexity, there is no way that purely physical dynamics could ever produce or be the cause or source of consciousness.[9] And as he often was, Whitehead was a visionary with this idea too. The belief that consciousness was preexistent or preceded matter in the universe is highly prevalent among our most expansive thinkers today, despite objections from the field of strictly materialist science.

If you're wondering what all this has to do with spirituality, here goes. When you apply the concepts and principles of process thought described above to religious and theological thought, you can see a philosophical basis for panentheism being established. Whitehead and his progeny recognized this too, and process philosophy sort of morphed into process theology, in which panentheism was a central unifying premise. The constant process of becoming taking place within matter could be understood as initiating with the Divine or Christ presence within all things, and preexisting consciousness or intelligence is from the Creator God and through the Spirit permeates all things.

So, as the title of David Ray Griffin's book *Reenchantment without Supernaturalism* suggests, there's no distinction to be made between the natural and supernatural, because the supernatural doesn't exist. What is divine and natural is in fact synonymous.

6. Griffin, *Reenchantment*, 53–57.

7. Griffin, *Reenchantment*, 6.

8. Griffin, *Reenchantment*, 97.

9. Griffin, *Reenchantment*, 82.

A famous quote from Albert Einstein beautifully illustrates all of this. "There are only two ways to live your life. One is as though nothing is a miracle. The other is as though everything is a miracle."[10] Einstein was another guy known for his big brain, so I think we can take these words to heart. The key is not equating miraculous with supernatural. Our creation, our universe, our reality, is naturally miraculous or naturally divine. I'm not sure if Einstein ever directly spoke on the topic of panentheism, but I believe that how he addressed it in these words is close enough. And that panentheism is an insightful, inspiring, and convincing way to comprehend reality.

Apocatastasis: Panentheism at the Back End

A related theological concept to panentheism/emanationism is apocatastasis, which is a Greek word meaning restoration, "to restore" in verb form.[11] It appears only once in the Christian Bible, in Acts 3:21, which in reference to Christ Jesus states, "For he must remain in heaven until the time for the final *restoration* of all things, as God promised long ago through his holy prophets" (NLT). In Christian Universalism, apocatastasis has also been closely associated with other verses such as 1 Cor 15:28, "when all things are subjected to him, then the Son Himself will also be subjected to the One who subjected all things to Him, so that God may be all in all" (NASB), and also in reference to the Christ, Eph 4:10, "and the same one who descended is the one who ascended higher than all the heavens, so that he might fill the entire universe with himself" (NLT). We'll see these verses again later when we consider apocatastasis in further detail.

Ultimately, our interpretation of apocatastasis is that it is the process by which all creation is fully healed and restored to divine wholeness in Christ, and eventually returns to exist in perfect oneness with the Creator God, "so that God may be all in all." Another way to describe it is that while emanationism is the creation principle of panentheism, apocatastasis is its teleological principle that describes creation's ultimate purpose, direction, and destination. Emanationism serves as the very beginning, and apocatastasis the very end, of creation's biography. All is from and eventually returns to God. A word I thought of that unites this concept is PanApoc, and if you

---

10. Rohr, *Universal*, 7.

11. "Eschatology."

think that's bad it could've been worse. My first brilliant idea was to call it EmanApoc, but I thought that sounded like a hair dryer or microwave.

An oft-cited scriptural reference to PanApoc comes near the end of the Christian Bible in Rev 22:13 when the Christ says, "I am the Alpha and the Omega, the first and the last, the beginning and the end" (ESV). Of course, many Christians have interpreted this as Jesus saying that as "the end" he, in human form, will make the proverbial second coming at the end of human history. What this interpretation fails to consider is that Jesus the person, even as the human incarnation of the Christ, did not exist in "the beginning," if that is thought to mean the beginning of the universe or the origin of creation. This Christ is the Christ of the Trinity, the Christ of creation, that "all things came into being through him, and without him not one thing came into being" (John 1:3 NRSV). As the Alpha, the Christ begot creation and existed as creation, and as the Omega, it is Christ that will draw all creation back at the end of time to exist in oneness with God.

What makes Rev 22:13 especially interesting is its use of the word "Omega," and how that was also used by a twentieth-century scientist/theologian who theorized that the end of time and creation will result in the universe's final reunification with Divinity. He named this event the Omega Point. We'll look further at this amazing human being in an upcoming chapter.

Chapter 2

God in Our Hearts
Historical Practice of Mysticism

As ALLUDED TO IN the introduction, it is reasonable to assume that the first instances of what we would consider spiritual practice in human history was through a concentrated focus on the person's interior essence or soul. Of course, since spirituality preceded the development of written language there is no way to determine this. All we can know for certain about any era in human history comes from written historical records, and to a lesser extent, archeological and anthropological research into fossils and artifacts. Some prehistoric artifacts such as cave drawings, carvings, and sculptures seem to depict deities and ritual activities, so those perhaps derive from myth and storytelling. And texts found inscribed on clay tablets from ancient Mesopotamia, one of if not the oldest civilization in history, described divine and mythological figures.[1]

Yet as much as common sense can be considered authoritative on a subject like this, it tells us that instinctive spirituality must have preceded any that relied on culturally created myth. Myth is much more conducive to written and artistic representation, so it is to be expected that we would find ancient physical evidence for it. Spirit or soul is notoriously difficult to draw, paint, carve, or write about, and it's easy to imagine ways of meditation and contemplation being orally taught throughout ancient history or prehistory before anyone decided it may be important to get this stuff down

1. "Mesopotamian Religion."

15

on papyrus. And even with that, some of the oldest, still existent religious literature in history came from ancient India and eventually became the basis of the Hindu wisdom tradition[2].

The more important point to consider here though is not what type of religious practice or worship came first, but to think about how the interior practice of focus on the soul and the Divine within may have arisen organically or instinctively before there was written accounts describing it, or even before it was widely taught from generation to generation. What makes this significant is how it may show that the inner quest is "hardwired" into our conscious beings. Maybe the divine manifestation of creation included a way so that the intelligent life that eventually evolved would have a link to spiritual consciousness programmed into their brains.

This is highly abstract, but let's look back to the previous chapter for a moment. If the creation we see every day really is a full manifestation or emanation of the Divine, then it gets a bit easier to imagine. If the spiritual and physical are fully merged and inseparable, that applies to organisms like us and our thinking apparatus as well.

If you look again at the title of this chapter there is likely an image that comes to mind, especially when you see the word "mysticism." It's of a bald guy sitting in the lotus position in some spectacular outdoor setting near the Himalayas with eyes closed and head slightly bowed, on the slow but steady path to enlightenment. And I'd also wager you associated this person with wisdom traditions such as Buddhism and Hinduism. We've all grown up thinking of meditation and mysticism in that context. That is the domain of our friends from the Eastern hemisphere. It is not something we do in the land of revelation.

So that is one reason why the rest of this chapter will focus on the less widely understood topic of the history of Christian mysticism. The other main reason is to illustrate the universality of mystical religion and meditative spiritual practices. It's important to know that this type of spirituality, what we're calling Group One, has been practiced and been a part of every culture and religion worldwide.

Christian Mysticism

In the big, wide world of Christendom, the fascinating history of Christian mysticism is often overlooked, despite it being as rich and extensive as it is

2. "Sanskrit Literature."

in any revelation-based religion. It remains an unfortunate situation, even if what's called the Christian contemplative tradition made a great comeback starting in about the mid-twentieth century.

Why has this been the case? Well, not to throw one of the world's biggest religions under the bus, but the de-emphasis and even suppression of mystical experience in the church really began with the rise of Roman Catholicism. Rome turned Christianity into a sectarian religion based on coerced adherence to a faith narrative, mostly by teaching (ordering, really) its subjects to believe in or worship a characterization of Jesus, not Jesus himself. What Jesus actually said and taught could be mostly ignored. Then by claiming ownership and taking control of this characterization or narrative, the church was able to convey to its people that they could only correctly obey God by fully subjecting themselves to its control. So, the sincere desire pre-Rome Christians had to understand and fulfill the divine purpose of their lives by following the example and teachings of Jesus instead became forced devotion and obeyance to an institution.

If that wasn't bad enough, the narrative people were forced to pledge total fealty to was nothing like Jesus's teachings and the essence of his mission. The church, with significant backing from the Roman Empire, told its followers that all they had to do to attain salvation was believe that Jesus's death on the cross was a sacrifice initiated by God the Father that allowed the sinfulness of humanity to be forgiven. The notion of eternal torment in hell for nonbelievers was brought into the mix, allowing the Roman church and state to create a powerful system that asserted total dominance and control over the empire's hapless masses. It signified the birth of the world's first theocracy.

This event, meaning the introduction of sectarianism into world religion, is one of the great tragedies in human history. I'm not sure if sectarian religion existed at all before the rise of Roman Catholicism, but if it did its influence has been lost to history. On the other hand, there was a reason the Roman Empire was known as the Roman Empire. Rome was in the heart of what became known as Europe, which was just starting to develop into the most powerful and culturally dominant continent in the world. And that dominance came to include forcing Christianity to every part of the world the empire could conquer and, as every student of world history knows, that turned into a sizable chunk of what was known as the civilized world at the time. The Roman Empire eventually collapsed, but Europe continued as the most powerful and advanced civilization in the world, and Christianity's influence and power grew with it.

This history lesson is included here only to show that Christianity didn't have to evolve the way that it did. It existed for centuries before Rome completed its takeover, and during that time it was a Universalist religion.[3] The prevailing belief, starting with the first apostles, was that Jesus's resurrection was the act that defeated death for all humanity for all time, so the earliest Christians weren't really concerned about personal salvation. They were much more motivated to prepare for what they believed at the time to be the imminent second coming of Jesus. And for them that meant to live as Jesus taught them, in loving solidarity with God and all others. So, from its inception, Christianity was much more a communal faith than an individual one. The emphasis was placed on being a loving and supporting member of the community, along with the other brothers and sisters in Christ. Yes, the early Christian communities certainly wanted to spread the faith as much as possible, but it wasn't because they needed to save people from hell or that God wanted all other faiths to be eliminated. That type of thinking was not at all a part of the original church.

The main point is that because early Christians weren't concerned about adherence to a sectarian orthodoxy, they were motivated to follow the teachings of Jesus, and not the mandates of a church claiming it possessed the authority of Jesus. And because of this Christianity had from its very beginnings a strong mystical element to it. The church eventually sought to suppress it because it didn't want people to know they could have a direct experience of God outside the prescribed rules of fidelity the church demanded. But in the beginning, like spiritual seekers had done all over the world and as Jesus taught, Christians sought to commune with God in the heart of their own being.

At this point, some of you may have questions about the link between Jesus's teachings and mysticism. Many of us who have grown up in the church are more what I call "death and resurrection" people, not "life and wisdom" ones. But all of us should know that the Bible has abundant instruction on seeking the Divine within, with a great deal of it coming from none other than Jesus the Christ. Furthermore, there is reason to say after even a casual reading of the New Testament that Christianity's first mystic was Jesus himself. In the examples he set, the words he spoke, and

3. Hanson, *Universalism*, 5.

the lessons he taught, Jesus was exhorting his disciples to follow him into the kingdom of God, which was described as existing within our beings.

This is not to say that Jesus wasn't the full human manifestation of the Christ, which is one of the church's core doctrines. But it is also church doctrine that Jesus was fully human besides being fully divine, and that distinction has made the life of Jesus inscrutable in many ways. All we can go on is what we see in the New Testament (and extracanonical writings if you're so inclined), and what is obvious is despite whatever divine attributes he possessed, his humanity compelled him to seek the Divine as well. This is seen not only in all the time he set aside for himself for prayer but also in how he taught his people to follow his example.

For most people, the concept of Jesus acting as teacher or exemplar doesn't attract a lot of attention. Much more consideration is given to the Jesus who could do really cool things like walk on water, heal the sick, and of course, rise from death. Being a teacher seems so ordinary in comparison. But when you examine the New Testament and look at all of Jesus's words and actions you can see that teaching was not ordinary or unimportant to Jesus himself. It seems as if almost every time Jesus said something or performed an action in front of his followers, he did so with the intention of teaching them something or being an example for them to follow. In fact, when one considers the amount of time Jesus spent being a teacher and role model compared to anything else he did, it's easy to conclude that Jesus considered that to be the most important part of his mission and purpose on earth.

As we know the Roman Church established the doctrine of vicarious atonement, meaning that Jesus took on the punishment that humanity deserved so that God the Father could forgive humanity's sins, and this was by far Jesus's greatest mission and accomplishment on earth. But one of the most intriguing things in all of Christianity is that Jesus himself didn't seem to think so, or at least he never talked about it. You would think that Jesus would have explicitly stated something like "by the way everybody, as the only begotten son of God I'm going to die on the cross for you and take the punishment for your sins so that God can forgive you and offer you salvation," but nothing like that appears anywhere in the Gospels, and ultimately it was centuries until the church established vicarious atonement as doctrine and an article of faith.

An example of the type of thing Jesus did often say though is in John 14:12. "Very truly, I tell you, the one who believes in me will also do the works that I do and in fact, will do greater works than these" (NRSV). This quote makes it clear that Jesus wanted others to emulate him and follow his example and that being human himself he knew that we are entirely capable of doing so. This in fact is what makes Jesus such an exemplary role model to us. We can see that he was able to achieve divinization despite being subject to the same human limitations all of us are. "Follow me," Jesus said on more than one occasion. Not worship me. Follow me.

So, what does this mean for spiritual aspirants who desire to do as Jesus asked and follow him on the path to perfection in Christ? Off the top, a couple of things. Accept that faith in Jesus means taking to heart his teaching that we can reach the same heights of spiritual realization that he did. Also, understand that Jesus himself was deeply spiritual and devoutly religious, and that is the example he wants us to emulate.

As mentioned before, it's easy to see in the "miraculous" things Jesus did he was indeed the incarnate Christ, the fully divine man. But also consider all the instances in the Gospels that Jesus is described taking time in solitude for prayer and meditation. Have you ever wondered what he was doing at these times? Despite being the incarnate Christ, it seems like the human aspect of Jesus also led him on his own spiritual quest. What was he reaching out to and trying to experience? That it's difficult to comprehend is an all-time great understatement. But regardless, I believe his desire was for his life to provide the blueprint for us so we could pursue the same spiritual perfection he attained. To put it another way, we should try to discern and practice the religion *of* Jesus, not the religion *about* Jesus.

Thankfully there have been many devotees throughout Christian history that have done exactly that. They are those followers of Jesus the Christ who were led on the same spiritual path he himself traveled, and they have come to be known as the great mystics of Christianity. They are the ones who learned what Jesus meant when he said, "The coming of the kingdom of God is not something that can be observed . . . because the kingdom of God is in your midst" (Luke 17:20–21 NIV). They also came to understand that the kingdom of which Jesus spoke is the same as what the psalmist called the secret place of the Most High as in "he that dwelleth in the secret place of the most High shall abide under the shadow of the Almighty" (Ps 91:1 KJV). The bottom line is, to interpret using the language of today, these places where the presence of God can be palatably and unmistakably experienced aren't really places at all. They do not have a physical location, or more accurately, they can't be found in a specific physical location. They are found within the consciousness through the ways of intuitive introspection and soul-searching that are more commonly known as prayer, meditation, and contemplation.

There are however a couple of issues for some Christians surrounding the topic of mysticism in Christianity, and they are mostly the concern of those for whom mysticism is unimportant in Christian faith and may even be of dubious validity. First, while there may be acceptance that mystical states of consciousness can be attained within the Christian belief system through Christian ways of prayer or worship, some people want to know if there are qualitative differences between Christian mystical experiences and those of other religions. This is due to the belief that practitioners from other faiths can't have authentic spiritual realizations like Christians have because they are from false or incorrect religions. The flip side of that is if there are no qualitative differences in the mystical experiences of different religions, then all of them must be invalid or delusional. This represents sectarianism rearing its ugly head again. Any spiritual phenomena that suggest universal applicability must be denied to protect the sectarian version of their faith.

Notes from the CU

When discussing the schism that was created when Rome seized control of the church and purged its original Universalist theology, it's important to assess not just how it affected Christian mysticism, but also the overall impact it has had on the faith to this day. Even today there are differing opinions as to what distinguishes Christian Universalism and mainstream Christianity. The prevailing belief may be that both exist on the same spectrum of Christian faith overall, with the Universalist and fundamentalist types sitting on the opposite extremes of it. But there are some of us who believe that the differences are not of degree. They are of kind. This belief asserts that when Roman Catholicism imposed sectarianism, eternal hell, and vicarious atonement on to the Universalist Christianity that existed previously, they didn't just alter the faith. They created an entirely new and different faith, one that was and is incompatible with the Universalist version that was ascendent the first four to five centuries after Jesus's birth.[4]

As a result, there is strong sentiment among Christian Universalists that it is we who are carrying on the original faith inspired by Jesus. In fact,

4. Hanson, *Universalism*, 11.

it has been suggested that Christian Universalism may be better served if its name were changed to Original Christianity, but the greater point is that we believe it is Catholicism and all the following Protestant iterations of the faith that should be considered revisionist Christianity, not the other way around.

But there is one thing that should be made abundantly clear. What Christian Universalism has in common with every entity that considers itself Christian is that we see in the person of Jesus the Christ the true reflection of the Divine. Even if there are Christological distinctions to be made among the entire church, Jesus will always be central to our version of the faith. Allow me to state without equivocation that the word "Christian" will always be included in what our faith is called, unlike some other Universalist churches you may be aware of.

In the next chapter we'll look at how mystical realization is reached and how our basic psychological makeup acts as an impediment to attaining these exalted states of consciousness.

Chapter 3

Realization and the Mind
Signs and Barriers

OF COURSE, THE TRAITS of true mystical experience are hard to describe. In fact, a defining quality of them is that they are ineffable. Even history's most articulate mystics have said using the language at their disposal to describe them is nearly impossible, even as they made valiant attempts to do so.

At least one reason for this may be that we use our intellectual and reasoning faculties of mind to process language, both in speaking or writing it and in hearing or reading it. But one cannot think their way to mystical awareness. It is not something that can be figured out, like how many more car payments you have left. It mostly seems to rely on how far you can get your mind to go into the interior depths of your being, before, behind, and beneath (what I call BBB) that upper layer of consciousness where you process your sensory input and manage your day-to-day life. You must extricate your consciousness away from your typical sense of self. Reaching this conscious state is called ego transcendence or ego dissolution. I prefer "dissolution" because "transcendence" has a spatial inference that isn't necessary, but I'm not a fan of "dissolution" either, even though it is the most commonly used term of scholars and researchers. The ego doesn't dissolve or disintegrate, nor should anyone want it to. A healthy ego is essential for basic social functioning and without one you'd be wise not to leave the house. What one should really strive for in meditation is to consciously escape their ego. The great spiritual teacher Ram Dass, who we'll consider in more detail later, phrased it like this: "The rational mind takes us a certain distance and no further, and we must be able to transcend it, to go on to other ways, other vehicles, if we are to cross the great ocean."[1] Maybe the metaphor that should be imagined here is that we're trying to create a doorway of consciousness that allows us to enter or exit our egos with ease, so "ego escape" is probably more accurate. We'll continue to use "dissolution" for the sake of familiarity, but I hope you can recall the easier, gentler image as to what is meant by that.

So, with ego dissolution or escape an essential aspect of the level of consciousness we aspire to, we can see the challenging task we have ahead of us. Even if I had the wherewithal to delve into Freudian psychology, it isn't necessary for our purposes, except to say it's well understood how dominant the ego aspect of mind is in each person's conscious experience.

It's a seemingly unavoidable consequence of human existence that as we age from childhood on, our conscious activity increasingly forms the mental construct known as the ego, the "I" that we present to the world and accept ourselves to be. From our earliest realization that we inhabit a physical body that seems distinct from the other ones we see, we individualize our own perceptions of being and attach identifiers to it that further distinguish "me" from "others."

My guess is this process starts as soon as the toddler stage, probably before we even know what our name is. It occurs as soon as we have experiences that we can attach value judgments to and assign them to the "me" that's having them. If the applesauce is great but the strained peas suck, you make it a part of your identity that you're a person that likes applesauce and hates strained peas. And as you may imagine, this process picks up tremendous momentum as childhood proceeds. You learn your name, your family members, where you live, and you start to consider yourself as part of a group that includes your family, hometown, and so on. This allows you to differentiate between other families and hometowns, but as the process continues you begin to identify yourself as distinct even within those groupings. Eventually we isolate our identities to the utmost. It's "me" and everyone else out there, and you create a psychological barrier that confines and separates you from all those others.

In addition to the inevitable construction of ego-identity or perhaps as part of it, there is the basic dualistic nature of human thought. When the intellect processes data it receives from the senses, it seems to automatically apply value judgements to it, like the strained peas and applesauce. I think

---

1. Dass, *Be Here*, 85.

somewhere in Shakespeare it says nothing is innately good or bad, it is just men's thoughts that make it so. Perhaps this is true, but what the Bard failed to mention is that these thoughts seem inevitable and unavoidable.

Neurologists tell us that the typical human thought process, whereby the intellect processes sensory data and applies a dualistic perspective on it as part of the creation of individual ego-identity, becomes cemented into our brain chemistry and makes our thinking become very inflexible and rigid over time.[2] This rigidity increases as we get older too. Eventually we all form what is called the default mode network in our brains.[3] This is what we wake up to everyday that reenforces and reconnects our ego-identity and sense of self, making our mental activity more and more repetitive over time. So, if you've heard the psychological maxim that we only use about 10 percent of our brains, this is what that refers to.

Again, I'm not a psychologist or a neurologist, but I am a theologian (that's what my diploma says anyway) and I understand the connections that exist between the psychological state of being and spiritual state of being, including the factors common to consciousness that interfere with spiritual or mystical realization. The point is that spiritual aspirants, particularly those seeking mystical experience, have a lot to overcome. The biggest barrier is that it can only be attained by far less prominent modes of perception. Instead of the intellectual/empirical level the brain usually functions at, courtesy of the ego-driven default mode network, the aspirant needs to access the intuitive level of perception. This is a serious challenge for most of us. This faculty of perception has been dormant for so long for most people that their brain needs to be retrained or "rewired" to make it work. Basically, being able to consciously exit the ego requires more than you may think.

Yet there is good news here. There is a proven method of retraining the brain that people reading this book are no doubt aware of. By mastering the arts of mindfulness and meditation, people have developed the ability to mentally bypass the dominant neural network the ego-identity uses every day to perceive the world. They can then access an entirely different realm of thought and awareness, giving them a very different perception and understanding of the nature of reality. This is what is referred to when it is said that the practitioner has achieved the state of ego dissolution. When accomplished meditators approach mystical levels of consciousness,

2. Pollan, *How to Change*, 328.
3. Pollan, *How to Change*, 301.

they say they are removed from their sense of self or ego-identity.[4] They're in a mental space of pre-ego-identity, as if their awareness has reverted to before they developed the personality traits and identifiers the world knows them by. They experience mental perception without sensing there is a "me" or an "I" having that experience or perception.

If you're wondering how we know this is what advanced meditators can do, you're asking the right questions, and here's where it gets more interesting. In the last few decades there has been extensive research on the nature of consciousness and how neurological functioning impacts it, and this research has brought meditation into the laboratory. Brain scans done on highly accomplished meditators doing their thing has shown them bypassing their default mode networks and accessing different neurotransmitters and sections of grey matter that are seldom used.[5] And as hard as it may be to fathom, using their brains in this novel way gives them a distinct impression of spiritual realization.

The bottom line here is that science has in large measure confirmed what mystics have been telling us for millennia, and that is human beings are able to ascertain and comprehend the spiritual realm of existence. It is unlikely that most mystics in history would have associated this realization with neural activity or brain chemistry, but it's not the "how" of this that's important. What is important is the unshakable certainty and conviction mystics have that they have attained an insight into this spiritual realm and experienced it as even more real than the physical realm of existence we see each day.

Have We All Lost Our Minds?

Uh, yes, but let me explain. When you have heard the phrase "lost your/their/his/her mind" being used before, it is usually to describe a person having a profound psychological crisis and can no longer think clearly or rationally. That's not what I mean in answering this question affirmatively, but I believe that phrase applies to all of us in a different way.

Everyone loses their minds at some point and it's usually early in life. It happens when we discover our minds uncontrollably jumping from one thought to the next, all day, every day. We don't control our minds; our minds control us. We then identify our minds and thoughts with ourselves,

4. Pollan, *How to Change*, 305.

5. Pollan, *How to Change*, 305.

which is the classic characteristic of ego-identity taking control of our consciousness, and we sacrifice our power to think intentionally. We lose track of our genuine, underlying self, which is our soul, our essence, in which we exist in oneness with God.

This is the main reason why when people first learn to meditate they are taught the art of mindfulness, which calls for keeping your mind as thought-free as possible. What meditation does for us, especially mindfulness meditation, is help create spaces or interruptions in our uncontrolled trains of thought. Our true selves can then regain control of our minds and purposefully direct them. What was lost is now found. You have trained and regained.

A basic teaching in meditation is to direct as much attention as possible to your breathing because we all breathe each moment of our lives, but many people find that challenging because their senses have nothing to be engaged in. An easier alternative for many beginners may be to practice sensory mindfulness and sensory meditation. In sensory mindfulness, one experiences a daily activity in their life, such as washing dishes, by fully engaging it with their senses of sight, touch, smell, and hearing. They practice not letting their minds wander beyond what they are doing in that exact moment and focus on how the water feels, how the dish soap smells, and so on. Even when you're just sitting on the sofa in a room you've lived in for years you can observe the physical sensation of how your back, butt, and legs feel while positioned in the sofa cushion. Sensory meditation is the practice of focusing and concentrating on a small object placed a couple of feet away, such as a piece of fruit or a candle flame. Again, the objective is to not let the mind wander to anything beyond the intended object of attention. Aspirants who learn to master sensory mindfulness and meditation first will likely find it easier when they begin to practice interior meditation on the soul/spirit.

Of course, these are probably the most basic and effective methods for most people, but when you start investigating meditation you'll see that there are almost as many ways to meditate as there are books on it. What's especially interesting is how writers describe meditation working on different aspects or levels of consciousness. Many guides seem to just touch on the surface of the benefits that can be derived from meditation, not that there's anything wrong with that, to quote Seinfeld. It's absolutely true that the psychological and even physical benefits of meditation make it very worthwhile. Many of us aren't aware of how physically and mentally debilitating stress is, and that stress results in large part not from the demands of life but from having an untrained mind to deal with them.[6] The positive impact of using meditation to train and regain control of your mind cannot be overstated. A person with the ability to live mindfully in the here and now and think intentionally will be flat out happier than they were before. But a person with high spiritual aspirations will recognize that is just a first step on the way to enlightenment. They've reached a point where they've gained a greater understanding of their true self or essence. They may not fully comprehend it as their soul or spiritual being but continuing the journey along that path will lead to that realization.

The Ego Thing

Having a strong, healthy ego is critical to having a worthwhile, satisfactory life. Without reasoning faculties, a person would likely not get past kindergarten. However, the importance of dealing with the issues the ego presents to people on the spiritual quest cannot be overstated. The mystical branch of every religion or faith tradition in the world emphasizes how critical it is to gain control over the ego.

Use of the word "ego" is a fairly recent development in religious literature, likely as a result of Freud's considerable influence. Religious texts and teachings going back centuries are much more likely to contain phrases like "I am" or "the self," but the meaning is the same, as is the importance of neutralizing its power on the path of spiritual realization.

One of the most significant tenets in Buddhism is that human suffering is caused by desire, or perhaps more accurately, caused by craving. There are many kinds of desire, and sometimes people desire to be of greater service to others or serve only to bring the will of the Divine into greater expression. But the desire that is the root of human suffering in Buddhism is that which only serves to gratify or aggrandize one's personal sense of self. These are the typical wants of human existence. It is considered perfectly natural to want more money, a bigger house, a nicer car, an attractive spouse or partner, more or better sex, anything that a person believes contributes to a more pleasurable and successful life. And in Buddhist thought, this type of craving is an inevitable result of the human person identifying as a separate sense of self, as we've described. In fact, a defining trait of the self in Buddhism is that of a being who craves or desires, and it doesn't take a ton of

6. McLean, *Soul-Centered*, 30.

self-analysis to affirm this. I am certainly willing to admit that I don't recall a day in my life when I didn't crave something for myself, even if it wasn't much more than an especially sumptuous lunch. When I was a kid, I had a constant craving for Devil Dogs (still love them by the way), but even more than the everyday things, I started to look forward to Christmas in February so that perhaps I could get a special baseball glove, a cooler bike, and so on. So, I would never dispute this basic tenet from our Buddhist friends: having a sense of self necessitates constant personal desire.

What's wrong with this? Why is this the primary cause of human suffering? Well, the top reason is this type of desire is never satiated. At best it's satisfied for a very brief period before a different gratification is needed and your life turns into an endless cycle of wanting something you currently don't possess. And no matter what you do have it's never enough, and your life is lived with a constant sense of lack.

How this problem is tackled in Buddhism is probably not how you think. Buddhist doctrine teaches that it is impossible for those with a sense of self-identity to eliminate desire, because desire is intrinsic to the sense of self and can never be removed from it. Instead, Buddhists teach that self-identity is a delusion because the self or soul doesn't exist in the first place, so desire is eliminated only when the sense of self-identity is removed in consciousness. The term used to refer to this doctrine of nonself is "anatta."[7]

That it's difficult for most people to wrap their heads around this concept probably goes without saying. Anatta is likely a unique feature among the major world religions. In fact, this doctrine probably accounts for the most distinguishing difference between Buddhism and Hinduism. A fundamental tenet in Hinduism is that every person does have a soul, self, or essence that is referred to as the "atman."[8]

However, for all practical purposes, I don't believe this distinction is all that meaningful. What's important is not whether or how one conceives of having a soul as their being's identity, but rather how firmly entrenched their separate sense of self is in their consciousness. In the mystical branches of Buddhism and every world religion, spiritual realization relies on one's ability to experience in consciousness their existence at its most fundamental or baseline level, independent of the traits or identifiers the world knows you by, and how you have come to know yourself as a being in the world. Whether it is called "ego," "self," or anything else, you must find

7. "Anatta."
8. Dass, *Be Here*, 86.

the psychological freedom from it to discover your soul or divine essence in the heart of your individual being.

The Christian Self and Mind

Does this idea of ego or self-dissolution come up much in Christian scripture? Yes, it does, though the language the Bible used to convey it is often so metaphorical its real meaning can be easily missed. What follows is by no means an exhaustive survey of Bible verses that can be interpreted as overcoming the self, but let's consider a few of the most powerful ones and see if we can make our way through the veiled language that often concealed their message.

One that has flummoxed Christians since there has been a Bible is in 1 Cor 15:31, when Paul says, "I die every day" (NRSV). On the surface, if there's anything in the Bible that's not a good recipe for healthy and happy living, it's this little tidbit from Paul. O great one, what could you have possibly meant by this?

While it seems obvious that Paul was not talking about physical death, we can take him at his word that in some significant way he intentionally experienced some type of daily demise, and he perceived it as a positive, spiritually beneficial event. Of course, as in virtually all the Bible this verse is open to differing interpretations, but as a practical matter what else can he be referring to other than his sense of self-identity as a being separate from God? At this stage of his spiritual development Paul certainly understood that at the essential soul level he was much more than a person born to time and circumstance. So, the "I" he allowed to "die" each day was his separate sense of self and ego-based identity. His spiritual essence emerged, and his self-identity was vanquished. He realized himself as a child of God and knew he couldn't be identified by how others saw him or how his place in the world defined him to himself.

"Whosoever will save his life shall lose it, and whosoever will lose his life for my sake shall find it. For what is a man profited, if he shall gain the whole world, and lose his own soul?" (Matt 16:25–26 KJV). This is a big one, and it has been unfortunately misinterpreted over the years, mostly due to the phrase "for my sake" in the middle. Many have understood this verse to mean Jesus wanted us to give up everything in our lives in order to devote ourselves to him more fully. But if the words "for my sake" are understood to mean at my behest or according to my teaching, a much richer vein of understanding is opened, one that is more consistent with the entirety of Jesus's ministry.

As Paul did with "I die every day," Jesus was not referring to physical death when he urged followers to lose their lives in order to find them. What Jesus meant was the human condition whereby our egos command our minds to the point where we identify with them while our true selves, our souls, go unnoticed, buried beneath the constant barrage of involuntary thought. We live our lives in service to these egos and believe we augment our identities through the pursuit of wealth, stature, and power. Some of us attain these worldly goals only to find they do nothing to achieve the soul satisfaction our real selves are truly seeking.

This is the "life" that Jesus implored us to lose so we can find the "soul" that we truly are. And we can see how well this message correlates with the one in Buddhism that says we must overcome all desire and craving for the material goods and physical gratification that can be attained in the world. It is only in finding the soul that the fullness of human joy and satisfaction is experienced. Jesus called this the kingdom of God and it's only discovered within human consciousness. The riches of the world and identification with ego/mind/thought can never offer it, only obscure it.

A quote from Jesus that refers to ego dissolution, albeit indirectly and with less clarity, is seen in Matt 18:3–4 with his statement "truly I tell you, unless you change and become children, you will never enter the kingdom of heaven. Whoever becomes humble like this child is the greatest in the kingdom of heaven" (NRSV). How is this about the ego? If you recall our earlier discussion on how ego/self-identity is constructed in individual consciousness, we saw how it develops slowly from childhood, as accumulative sensory data and continued identification with mind creates the impression of a self separate from the rest of creation. Each person is born in a pristine state in which they live more from their divine essence, but few if any people reach adulthood or even adolescence with that state of mind.

However, much of this original consciousness or awareness is retained by children as they maintain their childhood. This can be seen in their awe-struck wonder with the world and their amazement with new experiences. Children actually use more of their brains than adults and don't sense themselves being as separated from their environment.[9] Note as well how Jesus uses the word "humble" in this verse. It's easy to assume that Jesus meant this child he was with does not have an inflated self-esteem but consider

9. Pollan, *How to Change*, 325.

instead that Jesus was referring to how this child (and every child) has yet to develop a strong sense of self or ego-identity and their consciousness is much closer to its original state of oneness with God. It is the realization of this that Jesus called the kingdom of heaven. We'll consider this verse and the parallels between child consciousness and mystical consciousness later.

In the Bible the word "still" is often used to refer to a quiet, meditative state of mind. Jesus calmed the turbulent waters that were rocking the fishing boat he and his disciples were in by shouting, "Peace! Be still!" (Mark 4:39 NRSV), but clearly there is a deeper meaning for these (and really, all) words of Jesus. He directed this statement to the body of water he was in at the time, but what did he want it to mean to the people hearing or reading it? What is this stillness the Incarnate Christ speaks of?

The word "peace" provides the biggest clue, as a peaceful state can only be experienced within consciousness, and for Jesus this means we must "still" the turbulent waters of our minds to find the peace we seek. This peace is a gift of the Divine presence and spirit within, but it can only be experienced if we are able to turn off the incessant mental chatter that emanates from our false ego/self-identities.

Finally, the word "still" is an important part of a verse from Psalms that has become very popular among spiritual aspirants, to the point where it is now often seen on T-shirts, bumper stickers, and wall hangings. "Be still and know that I am God" (Ps 46:10 NRSV) is now seen by many as the most complete one-sentence instruction manual for seeking mystical experience in the entire Bible. In seminary I often remarked to colleagues that if the Bible were to be reduced to eight words and still retain its most important message, these are those eight words.

Here, the stillness we looked at in the prior paragraph is put into service to attain a realization much more complete than just a peaceful state of mind. Of tremendous significance is the following "know that I am God," which shifts the attention to what or who the "I am" is. It is simple to imagine the Source and Substance of All Being saying that if you can just get your minds to cease its pointless babble about worldly matters, you can bear witness to the Divine presence right in front of you, in that very time and place. So, in that sense it is a call to see the Christ of Creation and understand that the physical world we live our lives in is also fully divine. God is the substance of all that is.

But critically, another interpretation is that the "I am" is what it sounds like when we read or speak this verse ourselves. We are each the "I am," and these words are emanating from within us from the God who also exists as our individual being. The problem is we can't keep our minds still long enough to have the realization we are one with God in soul and spirit. So, God, via the Psalmist, is shouting this message to us from within, to that which we sadly and falsely experience as a self separated from God.

This verse has always been dear to me because in it I see a definitive guide to the wholistic spirituality I've tried to espouse. God is everywhere present and there to be ascertained when we can see the world around us without distraction and when we can direct our attention within us to the soul of our being.

Chapter 4

The Timepiece of the Puzzle
and Some Other Things

ANOTHER THING THAT NEEDS to be considered in the general discussion about mysticism is that there are chronological and spatial elements involved in the experience of it. You've heard a great deal in the preceding pages about how the spiritual aspirant must psychologically escape their sense of ego-identity and find their pre-ego development consciousness, so they can rediscover the pure awareness they were born with. It is in this purely aware state that the separate sense of self is eradicated and oneness with the Divine in both the inner soul and the outer world is experienced.

There are, however, important traits involving time and place that are essential in both attaining and defining the spiritual realization we aspire to. *Be Here Now*, written by Ram Dass (the man formerly known as Richard Alpert) and published in 1971, has gotten credit as being the book that first introduced the principle of mindfulness as spiritual practice to popular culture. In 1999, Eckhart Tolle's *The Power of Now* was published and quickly claimed its place as a classic of modern spiritual literature. I'm of the opinion that anyone who has written a spiritual book in the twenty-first century likely has a debt of gratitude for both these great works. While the importance of understanding oneself only existing in the present time and place was described in spiritual circles well before Ram Dass, it may be only since his work that the concept has been widely disseminated and understood. In any event, what makes the concept of presence such a powerful spiritual tool is that it is ego-identity's greatest enemy.

The reason for this quickly becomes evident when one objectively analyzes the content of their everyday conscious thought. When our minds are controlling us (and we're unable to intentionally direct our thoughts), it is easy to see the most distinguishing characteristic of these thoughts is they always direct your attention toward what you have already experienced in the past or think you may experience in the future, usually in another physical location than the one you are in that moment. You believe you are thinking, but it is really your mind, which is *not* you, driving the runaway train of involuntary and uncontrolled thought *at* you.

Mindfulness is the practice of fighting back against this condition and putting a Jersey barrier on the tracks of your consciousness to stop the runaway thought train from proceeding (how's that for a metaphor!). Most people define mindfulness as keeping your consciousness as thought-free as possible and that's partially accurate, but the only way to effectively do that is to bring your awareness fully to your experience in the here and now. Total immersion in the present moment hits the mute button on the mind's incessant narrative on past, future, and someplace else. Ego-identity is nullified because it relies on compulsive thought on imaginary experience to exist. The word "imaginary" is used because personal events from one's past that are recalled are only memories. They aren't experiences anymore. Experiences can only be actual, meaning they can only exist in the present moment. And as the past no longer exists, what is considered to be the future is even more nonexistent, if that makes any sense.

It's been said that the future doesn't have an ontological status, which is a fancy way of saying there is no such thing as the future. We can imagine what may occur in the rest of our lifetimes. We can even plan for what we hope will be events to come. For example, say you've decided that you want to be a doctor. In that moment you can take the first steps in applying to medical school, and as you do so, that is your reality, your actual experience of life. The results of those actions can be imagined, guessed at, or hoped for, but those thoughts can't create an actual reality, because the moment of its possible manifestation hasn't arrived yet, and there's no way of knowing that it will.

So, as Buddhists define ego as that aspect of consciousness that necessarily craves or desires, it seems clear another characteristic can be added to that definition. In order to survive and maintain its dominant role in individual consciousness, the ego must direct its subject's thoughts and attention to past, future, and someplace else. It withers and dies in the face of a strong conscious presence in the here and now.

As previously stated, the part of consciousness that plans, analyzes, decides, solves, and reasons is essential to effective functioning in the world. The problem lies in how much that faculty of thought takes over one's entire life and conscious experience. The real you, the soul, is that spiritual essence that lays before, behind, and beneath (BBB) your everyday consciousness, just hoping for the chance to be rediscovered, so that it can regain control of conscious thought and live more fully in the present moment.

To say that Ram Dass was an interesting character is an extraordinary understatement. His amazing earthly life ended in December 2019 at age eighty-eight, but not before he left an impression and legacy in contemporary spirituality unlike any other. Of course, any responsible account of his life must include the period when he was known as Richard Alpert, especially when he was a psychology professor at Harvard and a colleague of Timothy Leary, whose name is likely more familiar to you. Leary and Alpert became among the leading spokespersons of the psychedelic revolution of the 1960s, and in much of the country they became symbols of all that was wrong with the burgeoning counterculture of that era. America clearly wasn't ready to accept a message promoting the positive benefits of LSD, psilocybin, mescaline, and other like substances, so Alpert and Leary were shown the door at Harvard and became societal outcasts. But Alpert was undaunted. He believed psychedelics opened his mind and gave him tremendous insights into the spiritual realm, and he took that inspiration to India, becoming a bona fide mystic and changing his name to Ram Dass.

It was the 1971 publication of *Be Here Now* that brought Ram Dass back into the public sphere, though it is safe to say that his new name prevented most people from realizing he was the same guy who a few years earlier was encouraging America's youth to try LSD. Regardless, *Be Here Now* is now considered a seminal work and a momentous achievement, marking a pivotal moment in the introduction of Eastern spirituality to Western culture.

It's a curious thing to pick up and read even fifty years later. Perhaps in keeping with the prevalent hippie zeitgeist of its time, at least half of its pages are in the form of what today would be called a graphic novel. Even so, pearls of wisdom flow off each page and show how Ram Dass had an amazing gift of using humor to impart spiritual wisdom unlike anyone else I've read. In one instance of this I learned a personal lesson of great significance to me, and in keeping with the theme of this chapter it had to do with the concept of time.

First, I must make a confession of sorts. I've always had a peculiar obsession with time or chronology. A couple of examples would be that I could tell you when a year or decade would be three-eights over, or the date I turned 33⅓ years old, that sort of thing. I think it's mostly because I've always liked to do little math problems in my head and time periods are simple enough to do them with. Harmless enough as mental quirks like these go, but as these last few pages suggest, not something a person seeking spiritual realization should be doing. So, I was very appreciative when Ram Dass made me laugh at myself and taught me something important at the same time. He wrote, "If you set the alarm to get up at 3:47 this morning and when the alarm rings and you get up . . . and say, 'What time is it?' You'd say 'Now!' Where am I? 'Here!' 4:32 three weeks from next Thursday?" Here now! "There's no getting away from it. That's the way it is. That's the Eternal Present. You finally figure out that it's only the clock that's going around . . . it's doing its thing, but you? You're sitting here. Right now. Always."[1]

A bit silly? Yes. But still powerful enough to give me a lot to think about regarding how chronology psychologically affects us.

One of the first things we learn as children is how to tell and measure time. Each day is divided into twenty-four one-hour periods, an hour consists of sixty minutes, a minute of sixty seconds. One can tell "what time" it is by looking at clocks that can be seen in most indoor spaces one happens to be. Days are kept track of by using a calendar, which follows 365- or 366-day periods we call a year. The year is divided into twelve periods of about thirty days each. These durations of time were calculated by determining how long it takes Earth to rotate on its axis and complete an orbit around the sun, and I think kids know all of this by the end of second grade.

Of course, devising a system for the measurement of time was one of the greatest achievements of ancient civilizations and there is no doubt it was essential to our continued progress as a species. But there is also reason to believe time measurement has intruded upon human consciousness in a way that distorts the perception of reality in significant and debilitating ways. People live their lives and determine their moods largely by what numbers say on a device in a room. It's 11:21 a.m.? Almost lunch time! Or 3:34 p.m.? Will this workday ever end? Friday? The weekend is here! May

---

1. Dass, *Be Here*, 79–80.

23rd? It's almost summer vacation time! There can be debate about how bad this is for the human psyche, but there is little doubt that our ability to live and focus on the here and now, as our spiritual leaders recommend, is very negatively affected.

I believe what Ram Dass and Eckhart Tolle would suggest is that spiritual aspirants try to live their lives pretending that the clock and calendar were never invented, and the passage of time never calculated or measured. It's a great idea and one can sense how psychologically liberating it would be. But our conditioned minds at the same time are telling us how difficult it is to conceive of. From this vantage point it seems as if a person would pretty much have to live in solitude like Thoreau at Walden Pond for it to work. Even if you joined a religious order and lived in a monastery, without access to television, the internet, or any types of media, you'd still have to know what time lunch was. I would anyway.

Still, how the concept of time negatively affects our perception of reality is clear. Tolle describes it with a story that asks us to imagine what would happen if we asked a tree, a dog, or any nonhuman organism what time it is.[2] Tolle writes that obviously the respondent would say something like "what the heck are you talking about?" It's now. It's always now. Now is all that it ever is. It's a great passage that illustrates how chronometry, or time measurement, is a human construct that we've superimposed upon reality, and is not intrinsic to reality itself.

At first my experience reading *The Power of Now* was not entirely affirmative. Tolle's repeated insistence on focusing on the present seemed to leave a lot out (I was reminded of the *Simpsons* episode when the kids demanded that Dad take them to the water park now, now, now, now, now, now, now!). I recall thinking that spiritual aspirants need to do much more than just realize their existence in the here and now, and it wasn't right to tell people that realization or enlightenment can happen so instantly. Even the Buddha had to sit under the bodhi tree a bunch of times! The necessary commitment means understanding the way ahead includes a slow, gradual series of steps. Patience, perseverance, and discipline are essential on the spiritual path, and it takes a lot of now-moments for aspirants to reach their goals.

However, as I read on, Tolle's message began to have more clarity for me. He wasn't telling his readers they could expect spontaneous enlightenment. He was explaining that one of the effects of an ego-dominant mind

2. Tolle, *Power*, 34.

was to be mentally trapped in what he calls "psychological time,"[3] which, among other things, tricks people into believing they need to do something, be something, or learn and understand something before they can attain enlightenment, and meeting these preconditions requires time. Thus, God-realization becomes an ever-elusive goal that can only be reached in an imaginary future. It's like when you go into a tavern and see one of those signs behind the bar that says, "Free beer tomorrow," and when you go back the following day you see the same sign saying the same thing.

Again, chronology is an indispensable tool in the world at large. If it weren't for our clock and calendar, we wouldn't know when we have to be at work, when to pick up the kids at school, when Christmas is coming, and so on. Yet when you consider it further, you see that in these ways and all others, chronology only serves and benefits the ego-identity, on both the individual and societal levels. In spirituality however, chronology is worse than worthless, or as Tolle explains, "You see time as the means to salvation, whereas in truth it is the greatest obstacle to salvation. . . . There is nothing you can ever do or attain that will get you closer to salvation than it is at this moment."[4] And how or why is that so? "You 'get' there by realizing that you *are* there already. You find God the moment you realize that you don't need to seek God."[5] Later, in emphasis of this point, he writes, "I don't call it finding God, because how can you find that which was never lost, the very life that you are?"[6]

Tolle's assertions are tantalizing, and I don't doubt they point to an objective truth. There is uneasiness even critiquing him, because after reading his work and watching his lectures on video, he seems to be a genuine mystic and enlightened being who writes and speaks with great sincerity. However, I believe that, in some of this great book anyway, he makes the way of enlightenment seem simpler than how most of us will experience it. It is not a psychic snap of the fingers away. Mindfulness still needs to be learned and practiced, and a certain level of skill must be reached before the aspirant can be fully immersed in the here and now without their ego interrupting them. Of course, when that glorious mystical moment arrives, it occurs in a definite moment in time, and includes realization of the now it's happening in. But in almost every case I believe the mystic has already

---

3. Tolle, *Power,* 56–57.

4. Tolle, *Power,* 147.

5. Tolle, *Power,* 147.

6. Tolle, *Power,* 224.

cultivated and strengthened their spiritual awareness to the point where the ego is incapable of interfering. A person without spiritual inclinations, and with a highly ego-dominant consciousness, will not have a realization of God just because he's told he doesn't have to seek God, even if he fully believes it.

However, it must be acknowledged that there have been occurrences in history of what can be called instantaneous enlightenment. People who have had near-death experiences have come back with a spiritually realized consciousness. Powerful psychedelic episodes have been known to precipitate spiritual experiences with long lasting effects. Finally, some people have what's called a dark night of the soul, experience psychological death of some kind, and come through it in a mystically realized state. We'll chat some more about dark night of the soul in an upcoming chapter.

Regardless, Eckhart Tolle has made an enormous contribution to modern spirituality by identifying the here and now as an indispensable element of mystical realization. What makes Tolle's work so powerful is how visceral it is and how it can be understood in such a cogent way. Let's face it, much of how the path to spiritual realization is described is vague and doesn't give people confidence that it's easily attainable. Saying that one must find their way back to the pure awareness of pre-ego development, where their soul resides in consciousness, doesn't give a clear picture as how to go about it. And to say that craving and desire must be overcome is not going to make anyone think, "Oh yeah no problem." But bringing the here and now into the equation makes the process easier to discern.

Self-Inquiry: Who Am I?

There is another method of meditation that many have found highly effective and is often recommended in spiritual literature, and for these reasons alone it's well worth examining. But of particular relevance for us is that it speaks directly to what we've described should be the goal of spiritual practice, and that is finding your soul, divine essence, and your true identity, which is obscured behind the mental clutter the ego creates to stay in control of your consciousness. This method of self-inquiry, of asking yourself repeatedly, "Who am I?" also has personal meaning for me which I'll share with you as well.

Sri Ramana Maharshi is the Indian sage who's credited with being the originator of this practice.[7] One day as a teenager in 1896 he was suddenly overwhelmed with an intense fear of death, but instead of pushing it aside he surrendered to it. He psychologically gave himself over to it and upon laying down underwent a simulated experience of death. He mentally experienced the death of his body but saw that something seeming to be his self was still alive. Thus began his quest to discover what was in him that continued to live even without a functioning physical form. He asked himself, "Who am I?" but instead of accepting the answer of "me, Ramana Maharshi," he asked who is it that is saying it is me, tracing back the question to whom did that thought or answer arise. He never allowed himself to be satisfied with any answer that came to him. He instinctively understood that before, beneath, or behind any answer that described what he was in the world or how others knew him was a distinct entity of formless essence, of silent awareness, that constituted his being. He was that silence of which all thoughts arose and in which all thoughts disappeared, and that he shared this pure being with all others and the Source and Substance of All Being as well.[8] He said, "Let him find out to whom are the thoughts. Where from do they arise? They must spring up from the conscious self. Apprehending it even vaguely helps the extinction of the ego. Thereafter the realization of the one Infinite Existence becomes possible."[9]

Maharshi is one of the great sages who wrote and published next to nothing of his philosophy or spiritual methodology. The only significant published work he participated in was the result of an interview he gave in 1902 to Indian scholar Sri Sivaprakasam Pillai that was published in 1923. In it he expounded on his method of self-inquiry and was insistent it was the only sure way of attaining self-realization and the understanding that what we are in essence is "pure awareness" and that "the nature of Awareness is Being-Consciousness-Bliss." He also said, "As all living beings desire to be happy always . . . in order to gain that happiness which is one's nature . . . one should know one's self. For that, the path of knowledge, the inquiry of the form 'Who am I' is the principal means."[10] By repeatedly asking oneself that question and rejecting all answers that come from "me" or the ego, the mind will eventually be able to stay in its source, which he

7. Maharshi, "Death Experience."
8. Maharshi, "Who Am I?"
9. Maharshi, "Instructions," para. 2.
10. Maharshi, "Who Am I?," 3.

identified as the heart. "When the mind stays in the Heart, the 'I' which is the source of all thoughts will go, and the Self which ever exists will shine" and "all will appear as of the nature of Siva (God)."[11]

There is a lot to digest when considering Maharshi and his time-honored pathway to enlightenment. The first thing is to acknowledge that the methodology is unique and distinctly different from any other that I'm familiar with. But the goal and end result of this technique is the same as the others we've been discussing. The "extinction of the ego" is attained, allowing for the realization of our essential identity, our "pure awareness" or "Being-Consciousness-Bliss." Maharshi used different terminology to describe the mystical, enlightened consciousness he arrived at, but it is essentially the same thing as others have experienced it. Feel free to substitute the word "soul" for "awareness" if that is an aid in understanding, or Jesus's "kingdom of God" for "the one Infinite Existence."

As far as personal meaning goes, yes, it is there, and it's also deep and intense. It takes me back to my early childhood. I doubt I could have been more than six years old. I have a distinct memory of sitting alone in my room pondering my life and identity. And as I was sitting there, absorbed in introspection, I remember repeatedly asking myself who I was, and knowing without a doubt that I wasn't just Peter Stilla, my parents' son, my sisters' brother, a child in my hometown, a student at the local grade school, or anything anyone outside of that room would identify me as. I just knew I was something much deeper than that and I wasn't going to stop searching until I discovered what that was. Actually, "rediscovered" is a better word. I recall thinking that prior to this experience I was fully cognizant of my soul, my essential baseline being, and it was where I knew God. But at the time I couldn't feel it or abide in it. I had let it get obscured and clouded over by my earthly identifiers.

I get that this may seem fantastic to some people. Are some of us what are called "old souls" and are somehow born with deeper wisdom or curiosity than others? Or is this just something more typical in the childhood of a person who would be writing a book like this several decades later? I just know that I had this experience and to show how distinct my memory is of it, I clearly recall I was sitting on the floor by my closet at the time.

I have no idea how long I was sitting there, but finally, at a certain point I felt something click, for lack of better words to describe it. There it was again, my soul, my spirit, my God. And I felt a tremendous sense of

11. Maharshi, "Who Am I?"

relief. I resolved right away that I'd never lose track of it again, but of course, human existence intervened. We all grow up, grow older, and years and years of sensory input and ego construction overwhelm the pure innocence and pristine consciousness of childhood. Yet I sit here today fully aware it is the purpose of a lifetime, and I believe all our lifetimes, to make our way back to the pure essence of being we were born with.

In our next chapter we're going to expand on our discussion of mystical experience by looking at what are called the five stages of mysticism.

Chapter 5

The Stages on the Mystical Way and How Some Have Arrived

THE FIRST THING NEEDING clarification is that the five stages of mysticism is a dynamic list. What the actual stages are called and if there are even five of them depends on who is asked, but in most cases it is only the terminology that differs.

What could be considered the canonical list of stages isn't firmly established, especially within the Christian tradition, but there is one that, following a modest amount of research, turns up most prominently and is as close to a consensus as we are likely to get. That is the one created by one of the greatest scholars of mysticism of the twentieth century, the great Evelyn Underhill. She was a prolific writer but best known for her work *Mysticism: A Study of the Nature and Development of Man's Spiritual Consciousness*, published in 1911.

If you're not familiar with Underhill, you're not alone, despite her high standing in religious scholarship. This is because despite her brilliance, her style of writing made much of her work difficult to read. She could be stodgy and opaque at times, making her ideas not as accessible as they should have been. Regardless, she was one of the most influential religious writers of her generation, as much as some of her better-known contemporaries like William James.

Before jumping into this, it is important to make the distinction between those committing to the mystical way and those starting a meditation practice with more modest ambitions. The large majority of people who meditate only want to tame their ego consciousness a bit. They want to be able use their minds more intentionally, gain control over the ego's constant stream of unwanted thought and have more serenity in their lives. This is great and mindfulness meditation is absolutely the best way to accomplish this. But these people will not experience the stages of mysticism we'll be discussing. These are reserved for the people who meditate for spiritual development and understanding or are seeking enlightenment.

Underhill described the five stages of mysticism in this order: Awakening or conversion, self-knowledge or purgation/purification, illumination, surrender or the dark night of the soul, and union and the unitive life.[1] The awakening occurs when the person accepts that there is more to life than how they have been experiencing it. They realize the physical realm is not all there is to existence, nor is ego-identity all there is to personal being. There is a divine/spiritual realm coexisting with the physical one, and ego consciousness only conceals our true essence or identity. So, there is an understanding that God is calling us to come to a greater realization of what reality is in its entirety, and "in the mystic . . . it means the first emergence of that genius for the Absolute which is to constitute his distinctive character."[2] This is not the full experience of the Divine, but it is the opening of the window that's been separating the person from it. He or she then understands that being on the other side of that window is the preeminent purpose of human life.

Purgation/purification quickly follows the awakening and occurs when the person realizes how entrenched and attached they are to the physical world and how imprisoned their souls have been by self-centered, egocentric living. This is a time of deep self-examination and reflection along with the determination to find and remove all the ego-based thoughts, desires, and behaviors that have blocked their spiritual progress, or as Underhill put it, "a getting rid of all those elements of normal experience which are not in harmony with reality: of illusion, evil, imperfection of every kind."[3]

The third stage is illumination, and as its name suggests, it includes the psychic dive through the open window into the sunshine of spiritual

1. Underhill, *Mysticism*, 203.
2. Underhill, *Mysticism*, 214.
3. Underhill, *Mysticism*, 240.

realization. You are no longer just believing in and striving for a taste of divine reality, you are partaking of and experiencing it. Underhill called it the "lifting of consciousness from a self-centered to a God-centered world."[4] We'll delve deeper into the insights and revelations that come from attaining illumination, but at a minimum the illumined person is drawn heart and soul into God's loving presence, gains with absolute certainty the knowledge of the spiritual realm of existence, and can personally commune with the Divine.

Sounds great, right? Well, it is great! A person who reaches this stage can consider themselves a bona fide mystic. But there are two stages left to go. What's up with that? Well as it turns out the complete mystical journey includes two plateaus. The illumination stage itself is a tremendous achievement and it's not surprising a lot of people stop right there, perhaps because they have a hard time conceiving there is a level of spiritual consciousness more elevated than the one they are in. But for whatever reason, they are content to alternate between mystical consciousness and that which the rest of the world considers normal, everyday consciousness. If there is a risk in reaching this stage and not progressing past it, it may be the mystical state would fade a bit and become harder to return to, but that is from the perspective of someone on the outside looking in.

Still, it's easy to imagine challenges in maintaining this psychic balancing act. It can't be simple to be in a conscious state of mystical realization and relate to loved ones and the outside world at the same time. Maybe the ineffability of mystical consciousness prevents them from conveying what their experience is like. But whatever possible problems illumination presents are miniscule compared to its glorious, transformative effects. Part of the experience is that it instills in people a deep love and compassion for humanity and all creation, and they are able to impart their experience with loved ones so they can vicariously share in its qualities. Some of history's greatest art and literature was created by mystics and inspired by their experience.[5]

Then according to Underhill, mystics who want to progress past the illumination stage must go through a dark night of the soul. Sounds a bit creepy, eh? It's even creepier reading about it. It is what awaits those most intrepid spiritual seekers after they reach the illumination stage. As momentous as that is, something is telling them that their journey isn't complete.

4. Underhill, *Mysticism*, 281.

5. Stahl, *Most Surprising*, 45.

46

They know that they have more work to do before their self-identity, however they perceive it at that point, can be dissolved and their essence be completely absorbed into the Divine. They also quickly figure out what they need to go through to attain this pinnacle of spiritual achievement isn't very pleasant.

The first phase of this is understanding that illumination, as joyous and gratifying as it is, is still something that is experienced by a separate self or ego, even if it is one that's greatly diminished in their consciousness. And as this realization is made, illumination begins to lose much of its luster. Its joy and exhilaration start to fade. There is still the comprehension of one's eternal spiritual being and the divine composition of reality, yet there is also the perception that you are not fully immersed in it. You still understand yourself as an "I," a being metaphysically separate from the Divine All. And with this realization things go downhill pretty quickly.

First there is a compulsion to eliminate any attachment to self/ego that remains in your consciousness, or even any mental conception that you exist as an entity that can be thought of as "I" or "me." And if you've been through the first three stages of the mystical path, the only way to do that involves the enormous sacrifice of giving up illumination, despite the transcendent joy and bliss it's given you. The reason why is the last word of the previous sentence. There is a "you" that attained illumination; still a separate sense of "I" or self that reaped all the glory of it. And for the final union with God, that "I" must completely dissolve into nonexistence.

Underhill described this by saying the person must "disassociate the personal satisfaction of mystical vision from the reality of mystical life."[6] So, poof, there it goes. Illuminated no more, the person finds themselves afflicted with an existential despair in which they question all that they previously thought had or lent meaning to their lives.

It should also be said that there are different kinds or types of dark night of the soul. One, as Underhill describes, takes place in the still ambitious mystic after being through the first three stages of the mystical path. Other times it has taken place as an entity seemingly unto itself, out of the blue almost, without any preparatory steps taken by those experiencing it. One person who described it happening in this way is none other than Eckhart Tolle, and he told how it came to him very unexpectedly. His account is briefly summarized here because it is the most compelling dark night of the soul narrative I've seen in contemporary literature.

6. Underhill, *Mysticism*, 206.

Tolle writes when he was twenty-nine years old, he "lived in a state of almost continuous anxiety interspersed with periods of suicidal depression." One night, he awoke in the middle of the night with "a feeling of absolute dread . . . everything felt so alien, so hostile, and so utterly meaningless that it created in me a deep loathing of the world. The most loathsome thing of all, however, was my own existence. . . . I could feel that a deep longing for annihilation, for nonexistence, was now becoming much stronger than the instinctive desire to continue to live."[7]

At this point this is likely as bleak as personal narratives come, but then a thought came to him that shifted the energy: "I cannot live with myself any longer." This thought stopped him in his tracks as he reflected on what it meant. "Am I one or two? If I cannot live with myself, there must be two of me: the 'I' and the 'self' that 'I' cannot live with. Maybe only one of them is real."[8] This profound and intense realization caused his mind to stop. He then described feeling drawn into a seeming vortex of energy and "was gripped by an intense fear, and my body started to shake. I heard the words 'resist nothing'" and "could feel myself being sucked into a void . . . suddenly, there was no more fear, and I let myself fall into that void. I have no recollection what happened after that."[9]

What happened after that is Tolle woke up the following morning and discovered his existence had been completely transformed. He was no longer the suicidal neurotic of the previous evening. He had become Eckhart Tolle the mystic, who walked the city that day "in utter amazement at the miracle of life on earth," and for the following five months "lived in a state of uninterrupted deep peace and bliss."[10]

How's that for a dark night of the soul, resulting in a psychic rebirth into mystical consciousness? Pretty spectacular I'd say. Yet it does raise some questions, especially relating to our previous discussion. To start, Tolle in no way described first experiencing the three stages of mysticism Underhill indicated were a prerequisite to the dark night of the soul. It also isn't clear what type of mystic Tolle found himself being. Was he an illuminated mystic or had he attained divine union, which Underhill stated would result after having the dark night of the soul? Tolle stated that for the longest time he had no idea what happened to him, at least in a way that

7. Tolle, *Power*, 3–4.
8. Tolle, *Power*, 4.
9. Tolle, *Power*, 4.
10. Tolle, *Power*, 5.

could be described with religious or theological terminology. It was only after reading spiritual literature years later that he concluded the intense suffering he underwent that night forced his "consciousness to withdraw from its identification with the unhappy and deeply fearful self," and what was left the next morning "was my true nature as the ever present *I am*: consciousness in its pure state prior to its identification with form."[11]

So, it seems clear that the dark night of the soul is more than just one of the stages of mystical formation, particularly just the fourth stage of development. It is something that can certainly occur as an immediate precursor to mystical realization, but history is filled with accounts of mystics who never experienced it. Today it is not even considered a strictly spiritual event, nor does it only take place in one night. It has more broadly come to be thought of as a psychological phase many people go through when they realize their self-identity and standing in the world, things and qualities they believed virtuous and valuable, interests and activities they considered enriching and enjoyable, and the sense of self they've spent a lifetime creating suddenly becomes void of meaning and conviction. Moral beliefs or political perspectives come into question. You don't enjoy watching sports anymore. All the things that have made you the person you are no longer give you any sense of well-being or satisfaction. And how long can people go through this experience? It seems as if the key to emerging from it depends on the willingness to surrender to it. If that's not there, weeks or months can turn into years or decades.

However, returning to Underhill's conception of the dark night of the soul, we see how she believed it was followed by passage into the unitive life, meaning the final merging of your soul or personal essence with the Divine. This is the big kahuna, the pinnacle of the mystical path, the final destination of spiritual achievement, the preeminent purpose of human existence. She wrote "the self which comes forth from the night is no separated self . . . but the New Man, the transmuted humanity, whose life is one with the Absolute Life of God."[12] In this life there is "a complete absorption in the interests of the Infinite" and "a consciousness of sharing Its strength, acting by Its authority, which results in a complete sense of freedom" and "an invulnerable serenity."[13]

11. Tolle, *Power*, 5.

12. Underhill, *Mysticism*, 481

13. Underhill, *Mysticism*, 497.

Of course, Underhill's account is just one of many that have been reported in mystical literature, and we'll consider some others later, but in keeping with the discussion of the stages of mysticism, other questions have been raised. Chief among these is that, according to many of us with a strong interest in this topic, there seems to be a vital stage missing.

Um, excuse me, but aren't we missing something here?

Specifically, where the heck is renunciation?

Although perhaps more prevalent in the Eastern wisdom traditions, renunciation has been considered a necessary step in every form of mystical religion. Christianity is far from an outlier. In fact, some of Jesus's most demanding words speak to the necessity of renunciation if one is to follow him to the kingdom of God or mystical union with God. The most challenging, and baffling to many Christians, are those seen in Luke 14:26 when he says, "If anyone comes to me and does not hate father and mother, wife and children, brothers and sisters—yes, even their own life—such a person cannot be my disciple" (NIV). Of course, this is one of those verses that many people who consider themselves Christian shrug off, as if Jesus was just in a foul mood that day and could be ignored. But the Jesus who spoke those words was very serious. This is because Jesus wanted to be followed, not worshiped, and these types of sacrifice are necessary to follow him into the kingdom of God.

Is there a possibility that Jesus was being somewhat hyperbolic in this instance? Clearly Jesus was fond of allegory and communicated in ways that were both easily understood and open to interpretation. But to examine this further it may help to consider the topic of renunciation in a more wholistic way.

What is generally meant by renunciation across the religious spectrum is that there are features of ego-identity that need to renounced, rejected, or disowned by the person who aspires to mystical consciousness. What Jesus said in Luke 14:26 is, though much harsher sounding, not too different from what he said in Luke 9:23–24, which we've seen a lot of already. "Whoever wants to be my disciple must deny themselves and take up their cross daily and follow me. For whoever wants to save their life will lose it, but whoever loses their life for me will save it" (NRSV).

What does that mean for twenty-first century mystical aspirants? In order to find their way back in consciousness and rediscover their soul, their essential level of pure being where they are one with the Divine All, aspirants must renounce all the ways in which they've constructed their ego-identity and all those things they've identified with, and are identified by, in the physical world. As just described, this includes the beliefs and things of the world that you've enjoyed, believed to be right not wrong, and considered good not bad. You have to give up all your pleasures and value judgements if they apply to or derive from the world at large.

The good news is maybe in practice this is not as extreme as it sounds. It's important to understand the difference between renouncing something and rejecting or opposing it, especially for spiritual purposes. Allow me to go out on a limb a bit and say that Jesus really doesn't expect his followers to hate their family and loved ones. I believe what he really meant was that if one truly wants to pursue the way of the mystic to the kingdom of God, they have to entirely reprioritize their lives. They have to acknowledge they no longer derive any amount of contentment, satisfaction, validation, or sense of well-being from any of those things of the world they once did. They are all meaningless now. Love watching football or baseball? Meh. Watch the news because it's important to stay informed about the world? Not really. Exercising to stay in good physical shape? Gourmet food? Fabulous sex? Meh, meh, and let's consider this a little more. We may be pondering two different things: renunciation and renunciation lite.

A lot depends on what we believe is really necessary to seriously pursue enlightenment. Renunciation implies that the aspirant must completely withdraw from the world and live cloistered or in solitude. Renunciation lite suggests that serious spiritual aspirants don't have to go to that extreme. They can still have families, a job, and live fully exposed to the world at large, much like many of those who attain illumination. So, is there one right answer or is this one of those things that depends on the temperament of the aspirant?

Coming out somewhat surprisingly on the lite side are two of our previously discussed masters, Ram Dass and Ramana Maharshi. Ram Dass wrote, "You might think of renunciation in terms of some external act like . . . leaving family and friends to go off to a cave," but he considered renunciation more like breaking free of attachment to your desires.[14] Once that link is broken, the renunciate "no longer thinks that he is his desires" and can, theoretically, live amongst those worldly things and no longer be affected by them. Ram Dass also quoted Ramakrishna, who said, "What is

14. Dass, *Be Here*, 9.

the necessity of giving up the world altogether. It is enough to give up the attachment to it."[15]

Ramana Maharshi also suggested that withdrawal from greater society is not necessary, as long as the aspirant can practice with great diligence and discipline his method of self-enquiry, the repeated asking of "who am I?" Again, nonattachment is the key. Maharshi also didn't equate solitude with being alone in some cloistered setting. "Solitude is in the mind of man. One might be in the thick of the world and maintain serenity of mind; such a one is in solitude. Another may stay in a forest, but still be unable to control his mind. He cannot be said to be in solitude. Solitude is a function of the mind. A man attached to desire cannot get solitude wherever he may be; a detached man is always in solitude."[16]

OK, Ram and Ramana. Fair enough. But perhaps not enough has been made of the temperament of each devotee. Certainly, the mental stamina and self-discipline of each person has a lot to do with the ability to maintain nonattachment when one is continually exposed to the desires of their ego-identity.

William James, one of my all-time favorite human beings (along with Ralph Waldo Emerson and Shemp Howard) and author of what I'll call the greatest nonfiction book of the twentieth century, *The Varieties of Religious Experience*, seems to come down on the side of renunciation heavy. For those he calls "theopathic characters," he states "The love of God must not be mixed with any other love. Father and mother, sisters, brothers, and friends are felt as interfering distractions."[17] For James, a cloistered life offers significant advantages to the aspirant. Environments such as those offered by hermitages and monasteries are able "to unify the life, and simplify the spectacle presented to the soul. A mind extremely sensitive to inner discords will drop one external relation after another, as interfering with the absorption of consciousness in spiritual things. Amusements must go first, then conventional 'society,' then business, then family duties, until at last seclusion," so that the practice of "stated religious acts is the only thing that can be borne."[18]

We have quite a difference of opinion here, though it's worth noting that James undertook his work strictly as an objective psychologist; he

15. Dass, *Be Here*, 9.

16. Maharshi, *Talks*, 4.

17. James, *Varieties*, 341.

18. James *Varieties*, 341–42.

acknowledged believing that he didn't possess the temperament to have a mystical experience himself.

Is it fair to say that after thousands of years of human civilization that the jury is still out on this important question? Yes, many of our most famous mystics came to their experience while cloistered or in settings that could be considered solitary or near-solitary. But there are others who were illuminated in settings resembling a busy street in Hong Kong.

Perhaps the bottom line, or what today's aspiring mystic needs to consider, comes to us from the brilliant Joel Goldsmith in his book *A Parenthesis in Eternity*. "There is a Spirit, but there is a price to be paid for it—a surrender. Spirituality cannot be added to a vessel already full of materiality. We cannot add the kingdom of heaven to our personal sense of self. . . . Our vessel must be empty of self before it can be filled with the grace of God."[19]

In a way, renunciation is to mystical religion what confirmation is in the Catholic Church. The renunciate is making a vow or commitment that they are determined to follow. So, to use Goldsmith's words, how best can they empty their vessel? How can they state without equivocation that there is nothing of value to be gained for my soul from the outside world and to renounce all those things the world offers and the ego-identity once considered desirable or valuable? It can be intimidating. It isn't easy to say that you are rejecting the conventional values of family, society, and the material world while continuing to live in it.

It should go without saying, but this is something the aspirant needs to be completely honest with themself about. If you truly believe you can pursue the mystical way while living amongst all the enticements and demands of family, society, and the outside world, and not fall prey to serving the ego-identity with its ideals and desires, that's fantastic. It's hardly unheard of! People everywhere are living this life every day.

It's fair to say, however, that the aspirant with a spouse or family would have to create the right conditions in their home life to pursue their goals. A spouse with similar spiritual objectives would be ideal, or who at least understands the psychological conditions the aspirant needs to thrive. Meaning? There shouldn't be a constant barrage of cable news blasting through the home. Ideally the television shouldn't be on much at all. Smartphones should be strictly for smart phone calls. Media exposure should be kept to a minimum. The living space should be uncluttered as much as possible.

---

19. Goldsmith, *Parenthesis*, 179.

Most importantly, there should be as much time reserved for quiet reflection as there can be.

Professional life is even more challenging. For most people this means eight hours a day in full engagement with the ego for the purpose of executive functioning. One doesn't just shut that off when their workday is done. The aspirant needs to develop strong compartmentalization abilities so that the ego isn't creeping back into their consciousness when they are meditating on the divine within.

What I've longed believed would be ideal for people with family and careers is, if possible, to start their journey with an extended retreat of at least a month. This would allow them to clear their minds of the worldly garbage and establish the right mindsets and habits. They can then return to their lives with a strong spiritual foundation and maintain nonattachment to the world. If you have this option, give it a whirl!

My Apologies, Evelyn

A bit much was made earlier of how Evelyn Underhill didn't include renunciation in her five stages of mysticism. However, as you now hear umpires or referees say when you're watching sporting events, "after further review," we can consider that indeed she included at least something a lot like it, even if she used different terminology to describe it.

Specifically, it is Underhill's stage two, the purgation/purification stage, that for practical purposes strongly resembles renunciation. Underhill described her second stage as when the aspirant understands all the ego attachments, value judgements, and worldly pleasures that have been entrenched in their psyche and must be purged if God or soul-consciousness is to be cultivated. Other words describing this in the Christian tradition are "repentance" or "self-denial."

If there are differences between Underhill's stage two and how we've described renunciation, one is how the former is more action oriented. She depicted the subjects, after deep and critical self-analysis, discovering what they need to do to cleanse their minds and hearts from the distractions of the ego and physical world and start to take those actions, so they can at least start on the path of mystical realization.

Just like, in many ways, renunciation! However, for us renunciation has more of a liturgical or sacramental element to it. Earlier there was a comparison between confirmation in Catholicism and renunciation in mystical religion that serves as a sound illustration of this idea. The renunciate is still doing all the things Underhill describes in the purgation/purification stage but is also making a statement or vow that they are committed to the mystical life and devoted to the Divine they are seeking.

This topic will be examined further, but now this is just my way of saying to Evelyn Underhill that she is still one of my heroes.

Is Meditation Overrated?
There's also Extreme Psychological Suffering

In the great cosmic scheme of things, it is likely perfectly appropriate that there is an aspect of the mystical experience that is downright mystifying. This aspect was brought to light when we looked at the mystical experience of Eckhart Tolle. This is the fact that sometimes mystical experiences are had by people who had no reason to expect them. They happen to atheists and agnostics. They happen to people who have never been religiously or spiritually inclined. They happen to people who have never spent a moment in prayer or meditation.

On the flip side, there are many people who have had meditation practices for years, have been devoted practitioners of spiritual disciplines like Advaita Vedanta, or have in some fashion dedicated much of their lives to the mystical path, who for whatever reason are unable to cross the conscious threshold to illumination.

It doesn't seem fair, does it? Yet, in considering this riddle, I've always started from the assumption that in our grand cosmic scheme things happen the way they're supposed to. Things are fair because divine justice is always at work. That doesn't make certain events less baffling from our human perspective, but if you're able to look at them a little deeper you might find at least some rationalization for them.

Case in point, Eckhart Tolle. His experience, as it turns out, is not that uncommon in mystical history. There have been numerous instances of people in the midst of extreme psychological anguish and for whatever reason found themselves almost rocketed into mystical realization. Tolle apparently had been very depressed for years until that fateful evening when it suddenly got a whole lot worse. Others have been in prison or solitary confinement. Some have been prisoners of war or in concentration camps, awaiting execution. In all kinds of extreme conditions causing people to be in utter despair, they, without a clue how or why, were psychically teleported into the mystic (thank you, Van Morrison). Why? Let's look at a couple of examples and see what we can learn from them.

Arthur Koestler was a Hungarian-born author and journalist who became famous through his best-known work, *Darkness at Noon*, a novel published in 1940. He was in Spain in 1937 working as a journalist covering the Spanish Civil War, when he was arrested by fascist forces, held as a prisoner of war, and sentenced to death. During his incarceration his execution seemed imminent a number of times and on one of those occasions he had an experience he described in his memoir *The Invisible Writing*. He came into what he called "a split consciousness, a dream-like, dazed self-estrangement which separated the conscious self from the acting self—the former becoming a detached observer, the latter an automaton."[20] At some point after that he wrote on his cell wall a mathematical proof that there are an infinite number of prime numbers, and his mind was seized by an overwhelming aesthetic appreciation of this human ascertainment of an aspect of infinity. He was reveling in blissful contemplation of this when he "noticed some slight mental discomfort nagging at the back of my mind—some trivial circumstance. . . . Then I remembered the nature of that irrelevant annoyance: I was, of course, in prison and might be shot," but then he recalled immediately thinking, "So what? Is that all? Have you got nothing more serious to worry about?" He then felt transported to a "river of peace" and was floating on it, when suddenly he felt nonexistent. "When I say, 'the I had ceased to exist,' I refer to a concrete experience that is verbally . . . incommunicable . . . yet just as real—even much more real." He felt "the sensation that this state is more real than any other one has experienced before—that for the first time the veil had fallen, and one is in touch with 'real reality,' the hidden order of things . . . normally obscured by layers of irrelevancy."[21]

In 1947–48, before becoming the president of Egypt, Anwar Sadat spent eighteen months in prison awaiting trial for his alleged involvement in a political assassination. He also wrote of his experience "in Cell 54" in his autobiography, *In Search of Identity*. He said, "In the complete solitude of Cell 54, when I had no links at all to the outside world . . . the only way in which I could break my loneliness was . . . to seek the companionship of that inner entity I call 'Self.'"[22] He undertook that quest in horrible

20. Koestler, *Invisible*, 350–51.

21. Koestler, *Invisible*, 352.

22. Sadat, *In Search*, 73.

circumstances. He was in solitary confinement in a bare cell ridden with insects with only a straw mat to lay on. Yet even in those dire conditions he discovered that "once released from the narrow confines of the 'self,'" his "soul would enjoy absolute freedom, uniting with existence in its entirety, transcending time and space." This led to "the achievement of perfect inner peace and . . . absolute happiness."[23] Like countless mystics before and since, he discovered "when the heavy shackles that had bound me to my 'narrow self' were removed, I began to enjoy God's love. I felt that I lived in His love, that love was a law of life."[24]

So, if there is one thing the examples of Koestler and Sadat have in common, it is the miserable, terrifying conditions they were experiencing. It could be argued that they didn't describe full mystical experiences, or that both men came to their transcendent understanding gradually, not almost instantaneously like Tolle. Tolle's experience also occurred in what we can assume was his reasonably comfortable home. However, of most significance is that all three men, and I believe all those who have mystical or near-mystical experiences while enduring extreme psychological duress or horrifying physical environments, were forced to withdraw their consciousness from their usual sense of self. Their ego identities and awareness had become unbearable, so they had to psychologically detach themselves from their sense of the "I" having such a horrible experience.

So, how were they able to do that? How did they, seemingly without effort or intention, do what many aspiring mystics are unable to despite having lifelong spiritual disciplines or meditative practices?

One answer worth considering is that "they" had nothing to do with it. Could it be that the God we share our individual being with, in its infinite love and mercy, projects its Godself into their consciousness to relieve the extreme suffering the ego is experiencing?

When reading these accounts, one can see a strong resemblance between them and many near-death experiences we've learned of, so it is easy to consider the possible role of the Divine within in both. Most of us have heard stories of people having serious heart attacks, in terrible pain and fear of impending death, suddenly having a classic NDE, which turns their heart attack into the best experience of their life! They are bathed in God's presence and immersed in divine peace, light, and love, and they emerge never fearing death again.

23. Sadat, *In Search*, 85.
24. Sadat, *In Search*, 86.

This is obviously conjecture of the highest order. But I think it speaks to the question of divine justice or "fairness" when we consider why some people have mystical experiences and many other people don't.

Does the fact that these events sometimes occur impact how we should think about the importance of meditation on the mystical path? No, not at all. There isn't a guru or spiritual teacher anywhere who wouldn't still insist that the intentional pursuit of mystical realization must involve some type of meditative practice. But as we look closer at the history of mystical experience, we realize that we may need to expand our understanding of how it can occur. One example of this is there is ample evidence that worshipful contemplation of the external or natural world can play a powerful role in spiritual discovery.

Chapter 6

Nature Worship *Is* God Worship
The Way of the Nature Mystics

IN OUR ANALYSIS OF mysticism, it's been described as a profoundly interior experience that takes place within the deepest level of individual consciousness. But as we learn of the different environments, both psychological and physical that it occurs in, our understanding of it broadens. As it happens, a very significant characteristic of the mystical experience is how often it occurs when the subject is witnessing and contemplating a beautiful natural setting. In fact, what is called nature mysticism is thought to be "the most common type of mysticism,"[1] and for what makes this important I'd like to refer you back to the earlier chapter on panentheism. If we are living within a panentheistic reality and the physical universe is an emanation of God, it makes total sense why many mystics have their experience in reverent contemplation of nature. They are perceiving the other aspect of panentheistic reality, the physical manifestation of Divinity.

So, while the aspirant meditating in their sacred interior space discovers God as one with their soul and individual being, the aspirant beholding and contemplating nature becomes aware of the Christ of Creation. And in many cases these worshipers don't even realize their reverence of nature is a spiritual exercise or practice. It's only when God as Creation is revealed to them do they understand the spirituality of their experience.

---

1. Stahl, *Most Surprising*, 45.

What can we learn from nature mysticism? First, it strongly supports the belief in the pantheistic nature of reality. Nature mystics perceive the Divine fully immersed and existing as creation/nature/universe. Second, there is a sense that nature is alive and pervaded with spirit in some way. This too is indicative of panentheism as well as panpsychism. Finally, maybe we should consider that mystical realization, in its most complete form, comes from recognition of the Divine both within and without. Perceiving God in or as the oceans, mountains, creatures, the earth, and especially in the hearts of others may play a vital role in the perception of God as your individual being, and vice versa. In any case having a nature contemplation practice can only further one's progress on the mystical path. So, our spirituality should expand enough to include that in it.

There are things about this type of mysticism that are also somewhat puzzling. First, as with the "psychologically suffering" people, it can on occasion happen out of the blue. It can also seem to happen to people without intent who appear nonspiritual and who may have never had a formal prayer or meditation practice. However, the words "seem," "formal," and "appear" are used in the preceding sentence because people who have a strong reverence for nature don't always think of themselves as spiritual because of that, nor do they consider their love and contemplation of nature as a form of prayer.

One question these events raise is if in interior meditative practice mystical realization is attained through the conscious withdrawal from ego-identity to discover the Divine within, how does that correlate with the contemplation of nature/creation? It's a very reasonable question, but I believe it has a similar answer. The nature mystics, even if they weren't aware of it and without intention, found themselves observing the world not from their ego-identity but from the perspective of pure awareness. This allowed them to feel they were a part of their observations and not a being separate from them. Let's consider a couple of examples of these events and see if we can gain a better understanding from them.

One that often pops up in spiritual literature happened to journalist and psychologist Wendy Rose-Neill, a British woman who had a love of gardening. While working in her garden one especially lovely day, she took a few moments to take in the natural beauty surrounding her and then felt an unusual impulse to lie face down on the grass. She then said, "The boundary between my physical self and my surroundings seemed to dissolve and my feeling of separation vanished. In a strange way I felt blended into a total unity with the earth, as if I were made of it and it of me."[2] This is a well-known trait common to mystical experience, especially nature mysticism. She went on to describe another one. "I felt as if I had suddenly come alive for the first time—as if I were awakening from a long deep sleep into a real world. I realized that I was surrounded by an incredible loving energy, and that everything, both living and non-living, is bound inextricably with a kind of consciousness which I cannot describe in words."[3]

English primatologist Jane Goodall is a name familiar to many of us and is known for perhaps being the world's leading expert on chimpanzees. Because her career has involved observing these primates in their African jungle habitat, she's spent much of her life deeply immersed in nature. On one of these ordinary days she had this experience. "Lost in awe at the beauty around me, I must have slipped into a state of heightened awareness. It is hard, impossible really, to put into words the moment of truth that suddenly came upon me. It seemed to me . . . the self was utterly absent. I and the chimpanzees, the earth and trees and air, seemed to merge, to become one with the spirit power of life itself. That afternoon, it had been as though an unseen hand had drawn back a curtain. . . . In a flash of 'outsight' I had known timelessness and quiet ecstasy . . . and I knew that the revelation would be with me the rest of my life."[4]

These two experiences are circumstantially different but metaphysically similar. The most significant commonality was the disappearance or loss of the sense of self, and the identity merging and becoming one with the immediate environment. Rose-Neill described blending "into a total unity with the earth," and Goodall described becoming "one with the spirit power of life itself," but both women spoke of their setting, and what they merged into, with great sanctity and reverence. Their worlds, their physical surroundings, had become infused and immersed with spirit, with Rose-Neill going as far as to call it a "loving energy" that's "bound inextricably with a kind of consciousness."

While the language used in these accounts isn't like that used in traditional, introspective mystical narratives, that shouldn't diminish how they are perceived. From our perspective these are authentic mystical experiences. Should we expand our understanding of meditation so that it includes creation worship or nature contemplation? Yes, especially if meditation is

2. Coxhead, *Relevance*, 30.
3. Coxhead, *Relevance*, 30.
4. "Mystical Experience of Jane Goodall."

understood as the one intentional tool for the pursuit of enlightenment. Any activity that's known to result in mystical experience as often as nature worship should be included in the spiritual practice we aspire to. It's definitely better than being suicidally depressed or in solitary confinement.

How does one develop their ability to contemplate nature in a spiritually insightful way? Much in the same way as in regular mindfulness meditation practice, the aspirant must, to the best of their ability, bring their conscious awareness into the presence, to the here and now. They must resist the ego's inevitable attempts to take their attention away from where they are, or to thoughts of the past or projections of the future.

Of course, bringing your conscious awareness into the here and now comes with its own set of challenges. One factor that plays a role is almost every adult gets out of bed each morning convinced there's no way they can derive any conscious gratification or satisfaction from their everyday environment. Heck, it's difficult for most people to stay mentally present when they're gazing upon the Seven Wonders of the World, let alone when they're in the living room or neighborhood they've lived in for years.

However, there is a powerful practice that serves as an entry point for the experience of presence and is fairly simple for most people to do. Sarah McLean, in her excellent book *Soul Centered,* calls it beginner's mind (BM), and she believes that it is not only an aid to accessing the presence, but also a necessary first step.[5]

To cultivate BM, one must commit to surrendering all that they think they know about objects in their environment, or "unlearn" about them, as I recall it being described. Create space in your consciousness so you experience things as if for the first time, even if it's something you've been in contact with countless times before. Discard any labels, descriptors, preconceived notions, or definitions you have stored in your mind about what you see before you, no matter how mundane or ordinary it may seem to be.

A problem with basic human consciousness is that it has accumulated so much data about things in its everyday environment that the mind is filled with it, and there is not enough mental space to have a direct experience of those things. Words and names for things that you hold in your memory are recalled, but the thing itself isn't considered or felt at all. You don't really see the tree you walk by with your dog every day, nor do you feel the outdoor air despite how pleasant it may be. You think you know everything you need to know about common objects or elements, so if there's

5. McLean, *Soul-Centered,* 51.

any mental activity accompanying contact with them, it usually involves just a fleeting thought of the name or word associated with it and then moving on to the next thought of some other time, somewhere else. Is it any wonder why for most people maintaining their awareness in the here and now is such a challenge? It's sad because people don't realize their out-of-control mental state prevents them from fully living their lives. They can be outside on a gorgeous day, not a cloud in the sky, with the bountiful life of nature emerging all around them, and their minds are still forcing thoughts of an upcoming oil change upon them.

There is a better way. Once you access your BM and put it to work, a whole new realm of life opens for you in which your ability to immerse yourself in the here and now is greatly enhanced. There are probably different ways of cultivating BM, and each person must find what works best for them, but the goal should be to find your way to a mental state in which you directly experience things as if for the first time. Whatever you think you know about something, such as what it's called, its classification in nature, organic status, or even if it's a plant, animal, mineral, or gas, do your best to ignore all your preconceived ideas about it. You'll discover that you can turn an ordinary walk in your neighborhood into a great adventure.

I was fortunate when I made my first attempts at practicing BM because it was autumn in New England, and there's no place on the planet I'd rather be. Right outside my front door I was greeted with a very pleasant sensation against my skin, and I took the time to thoroughly feel it and consider the degree of which it felt better than other times I've walked out of the house. I basked in and appreciated it without giving a thought to what was causing it. You've probably figured out it was the air temperature, even though I couldn't tell you what the temperature was. I just experienced how good it felt.

A few steps later I came upon a large thing that had burst out of the ground. It was at least ten times as tall as I am and there was no way I could put my arms around it and touch my hands. At eye level it wasn't visually pleasing. It was a brownish gray and textually very rough and creviced. Taking a few steps back though and looking over my head, I beheld a spectacular vision. Numerous arms were projecting out of the base and from these softer, thinner, brightly colored objects flowed through the breeze. They were mostly bright orange with some yellow and red mixed in. I allowed my visual sense to become completely absorbed with the experience for a while before my thoughts turned to consideration of the object as a whole. Why does this thing exist and share this environment with me? Does it serve a purpose other than being beautiful to other life forms who have the pleasure of observing it? I shared a moment of kinship with it, as it too is a manifestation of the Divine as I am.

A few more steps down the road I came into a clearing and saw in the distance many other objects like the one I just described, though the colors at their tops varied. Gazing above them I saw a giant arc seemingly painted a very pleasing light blue, with a few irregularly shaped and placed patches of white set against it. After taking it all in for a period of unknown duration I just stood in awestruck silence, trying to comprehend its magnificence. The one thing I recall thinking most of all is that it can't be an accident that our world is so naturally beautiful. The Source and Substance of All Being manifested itself beautifully and lovingly because that is the only way it could.

So, a few conclusions. First, being outdoors in a natural setting is certainly a great aid to this practice. While the same principles of reality apply wherever one is, it's fair to say that BM is more difficult for most people to practice indoors, unless you're Aldous Huxley and you've just eaten a fistful of peyote. Second, if you can fully activate your BM as you take your walk, you'll likely be surprised at how long you can stay anchored in the present moment. Ego thoughts of past and future will not arise when you are fully immersed and actively engaging with your environment. Lastly, after spending some time in this consciousness, you may experience your awareness transcend even further and become a more cosmic, wholistic kind of contemplation. The presence is nothing if not divine, and you will get a sense of God as the basis of all reality.

When I first read about and began practicing BM, I was reminded of another spiritual practice I devised that is similar to it in many ways. I never formally gave it a name, but I suppose a good one would be "never take life for granted." It acts as a daily prayer of gratitude to God while making us appropriately awestruck with our continued existence. It's good to practice in the early morning because most of us find ourselves being mentally burdened by the particulars of our material needs as soon as we get up. We think about what happened to us yesterday and what we must do today to pursue the demands of our egos and consumer life. We seldom give any real consideration to what would constitute our genuine well-being, even though I think most of us instinctively understand that should be our top priority. Instead, we all too often fall prey to the illusion that our "real world" concerns should take precedence over that which nourishes our souls and enhances our spiritual wellness. "First Things First" is now a spiritual cliché but there's still a lot of wisdom in it. We should be thankful every day that we exist and are alive at all. We should never lose sight of how incredible it is that we are here in the first place. It brings us back in touch with the joy of life itself.

Sometimes the burdens of life feel so overwhelming it seems as if they negate any positive things we can experience from it. We may wonder what is it that nurtures us? What is it that fulfills us? At times like these it may be wise to return to what I call the basics and consider what a miracle it is that we are even here to ask these questions. And when we do is when we never take life for granted. Most of us are familiar with what is called the big bang; that event fourteen billion or so years ago when astronomers and physicists tell us the universe came into being. Innumerable laws of physics came into being at that very moment as well, and if any one of them, such as the rate of gravitation, were minutely different, the formation of galaxies, stars, and planets would have been impossible. Closer to home, if our Earth orbited the Sun a short astronomical distance closer or further away, or if the Sun itself was a small percentage larger or smaller, life on Earth never would have arisen. We understand that human life is the result of millions of years of evolution, but how did purely inorganic matter come together to form even microscopic life? And how is it possible that any organism, comprised solely of physical elements, has consciousness, which allows us to think, feel, and be truly alive?

What puts me in a state of awe and amazement when I think about it are the astronomical details of this planet we call home. We live on a giant sphere that makes a complete rotation on its axis every twenty-four hours. While this is happening, the sphere is also orbiting a tremendous energy source about ninety-three million miles away that makes all life on our planet possible. One complete orbit takes 365 of those twenty-four hour periods we call days. And it does all of this in such an orderly way, we are able to determine the exact time, down to the second, when this energy source will first become visible each day to people living at every point on the sphere, and the time each day when it dips out of sight. We also know with the same precision the path of our orbit, which determines when our energy source is most directly affecting the top and bottom halves of our sphere and creates the periods of time we call the seasons each year.

I understand that all of us who have been fortunate enough to have received a decent education knows these things. But what turns intellectual knowledge into prayer or spiritual practice is when we take the time to reflect on these things and really feel them. Yes, it's second nature for us to immediately get into our ego/logical/empiricist consciousness each day, as we strive to meet our work or family responsibilities. But please, take some time to first contemplate our creation, our ultimate reality in which all those mundane tasks take place.

What I believe makes this a powerful spiritual practice is that it, like beginner's mind, brings our attention back to the essential, foundational realities of being. BM works on the sensory input we receive each day and makes us reconsider it without the labels we previously applied to it through our logic and reasoning. We're forced to fully engage with it and experience it in the here and now, where the ego is incapable of intervening. Reality/nature is processed at the soul level, and the divine imprint is more easily discerned.

Never take life for granted works mostly with the reality beyond the reach of our senses, and perhaps, depends on the subject having a modicum of knowledge in science or astronomy. But it still directs our attention to the ultimate and absolute, and our consciousness is infused with awe and wonderment. Creation is more easily seen in the light of the Divine and synonymous with God, as panentheism suggests that it should. Most importantly, we see ourselves belonging to, and a product of, creation in a profound way. We get the sense that the power that created and sustains us, while ensuring Earth is rotating and orbiting in the heavens precisely as it should, doesn't want us worried by an unexpected bill.

Next, we're going to consider some of the qualities of mystical experience. Despite their supposed ineffability, there are still traits by which they can be identified and spiritual lessons that can be learned from them.

Chapter 7

Realization of the One
The Qualities and Lessons of Mysticism

To this point we have considered the stages one may go through and steps that may need to be taken on the mystical path. We've also looked at how mystical realization is attained, in most cases intentionally but often unintentionally, resulting from extreme psychological duress or worshipful contemplation of nature. But instead of how mystical experiences are arrived at, we'll now consider what they're like while people are having them. What feelings do they engender? What characteristics do they have that truly qualify them as being mystical, and not just insightful, healing or personally rewarding? What lessons have been or can be learned from them, both by the subject and those who study them?

We'll first look at what some of the great religious writers have said about these aspects of mysticism so we can consider the perspective of scholarly thought. Mostly though, despite the opinion expressed by many that mystical experience is ineffable or indescribable, we're going to look at some excerpts of mystics conveying to the best of their ability their experiences in their words. Because really, there are degrees of "ineffable." In one sense the word applies to mystical experience in its entirety because it occurs in an area of consciousness where both language and logic are inadequate for the task. However, there are many mystics who have been able to eloquently describe what they feel they have ascertained from their experiences. There is in mystical literature numerous accounts of conclusions drawn, understandings reached, and lessons learned, even if descriptions of what would substantiate those conclusions often exceeds the scope of human communication.

There are several reasons to do this. Besides just for our edification, these accounts will be very inspirational and validating to every spiritual seeker and for that reason alone including them is worthwhile. It is easy to see that these narratives describe the greatest, most rewarding and fulfilling conscious experiences a human being can possibly have. So, yeah, let's delve into these a bit! We'll also look at how these experiences tie into some of the psychological and theological factors we've discussed already. Among these is that reality is perceived as fully Divine and existing as oneness, a singularity without differentiation. Time and space are seen as illusory, as mystics see reality only occurring in what's referred to as an eternal here and now. Finally, we'll see how mystics describe their experiences as taking place outside the confines of their ego-identity and usual dualistic mode of thought.

James and Underhill again, and introducing Richard Maurice Bucke

We'll start with William James, who considered himself a scientist and psychologist, and not religious in any meaningful way. *The Varieties of Religious Experience* was one of if not the first truly objective and scientific treatments of religious phenomena, which is why it has been so influential over the years. He didn't have an agenda to substantiate or discredit religious experience when researching the book, and you may get the distinct impression upon reading it he may been surprised by what he discovered.

In the section on mysticism, James described four distinct characteristics by which the experience can be identified.[1] The first is the oft-mentioned ineffability, and he states, "The subject of it immediately says that it defies expression, that no adequate report of its content can be given in words."[2] Second is what he called their "noetic quality," meaning "mystical states seem to those who experience them to be also states of knowledge. They are states of insights into the depths of truth unplumbed by the discursive intellect. They are illuminations, revelations, full of significance and importance."[3] Third, they can be known by their transiency. Only rarely do

1. James, *Varieties*, 371.

2. James, *Varieties*, 371.

3. James, *Varieties*, 371.

they last longer than an hour or two. Lastly, they are known by their passivity. When they occur, "the mystic feels as if his own will were in abeyance, and indeed sometimes as if he were grasped and held by a superior power."[4]

To twenty-first-century readers of religious literature this list may not seem that remarkable. Indeed, we will see some of these characteristics described from the "inside," by those who have been in mystical states. But what makes the list noteworthy is that it represents an objective substantiation of mysticism from a scientific field of study for the first time ever, now 120 years after its publication.

We'll go again now to Evelyn Underhill. While William James gave us the scientific/logical perspective, Underhill will give us that of the deeply religious/logical. She had a foot in both worlds. She was a prolific writer and tremendous scholar, but her religious convictions allowed her intuitive gifts to come out in her work. Second, she may have seen herself as being an intellectual or academic rival to William James. When she wrote *Mysticism*, her list of the characteristics of mysticism was said to be in part an intentional refutation of James's list, which she apparently didn't think very highly of.[5]

Right off the bat Underhill writes, "True mysticism is active and practical, not passive and theoretical. It is an organic life process, a something which the whole self does; not something as to which its intellect holds an opinion."[6] James's fourth characteristic, passivity, is directly contradicted. For some of us, especially non-mystics, this is a hard one to fathom. The more common conception of mystical experience is that while the subject may arrive at that conscious state through prayer or meditation, the experience happens *to* him or her. It isn't something that is self-directed. Maybe in the big scheme of things this is a minor point, but it may be an example of Underhill's religious sensibilities leading her to this conclusion.

Second, she says of mysticism, "Its aims are wholly transcendental and spiritual," and not at all concerned with "anything in the visible universe." To this though she adds a significant addendum. "The mystic . . . does not, as his enemies declare, neglect his duty to the many, his heart is always set upon the changeless One."[7] There is amongst those of more orthodox

4. James, *Varieties*, 372.

5. Milos, "Underhill's Mysticism."

6. Underhill, *Mysticism*, 96.

7. Underhill, *Mysticism*, 96.

religious thought a sentiment that the mystical path is a selfish spiritual pursuit, but here Underhill directly refutes that idea.

Third, Underhill writes, "This One," and for her the word "One" must be considered synonymous with God or ultimate reality, "is for the mystic, not merely the Reality of all that is, but also a living and personal Object of Love."[8] This is where Underhill starts to truly distinguish herself from James. James made a cursory and objective reference to "a superior power" in his list, but Underhill dives deeply into that superior power and how the mystic experiences and has communion with it. "It" is also described as principle and personal and the mystic enters into a love relationship with it. For this characteristic, Underhill blurs the line somewhat between a scholarly observation and the perspective of the experiencer.

In her last characteristic, Underhill describes the unitive state, the final destination on the mystical path, and she seems to blend her description here with the depiction of the unitive state in her five stages of mysticism. She writes that "it is arrived at by an arduous psychological and spiritual process—the so-called Mystic Way—entailing the complete remaking of character and the liberation of a new, or rather latent, form of consciousness."[9] Note that the "arduous process" seems to confirm her description of the five stages. But as if to make undoubtedly clear this is a metaphysical event, she continues, "It is the name of that organic process which involves the perfect consummation of the Love of God; the achievement here and now of the immortal heritage of man . . . the art of establishing a conscious relation with the Absolute."[10]

As we move on to the personal accounts of the mystics themselves, we're also moving from the characteristics of mysticism to the lessons and understandings that are derived from the experience. As we'll see, these narratives aren't concerned with defining it in any way. Instead, they tell of the circumstances, insights, and awesome power of the experience.

We'll start with Richard Maurice Bucke, who with James and Underhill formed what could be called the Big Three of early twentieth-century mysticism and religious scholarship. His book *Cosmic Consciousness* was published a year before *The Varieties of Religious Experience* and was also a remarkable contribution to the theology of mysticism. An interesting tidbit about the book is that its title became a synonym for its subject. "Cosmic

8. Underhill, *Mysticism*, 96.
9. Underhill, *Mysticism*, 96.
10. Underhill, *Mysticism*, 97.

consciousness" is now used the same way as other words and phrases like "mystical realization" and "enlightenment," among others. Most significantly, Bucke was himself a mystic, and his personal experience is described in the book.

He was going home in a hansom cab following a pleasant evening with friends, discussing romantic poetry and other topics, and was feeling enthralled and intellectually stimulated by the events of the evening. Suddenly, "he found himself wrapped around as it were by a flame-colored cloud . . . directly afterwards came upon him a sense of exultation, of immense joyousness . . . followed by an intellectual illumination quite impossible to describe." However, in this experience, "he saw and knew that the Cosmos is not dead matter but a living presence, that the soul of man is immortal, that the universe is so built and ordered that without any peradventure all things work together for the good of each and all, that the foundation principal of the world is what we call love and that the happiness of every one is in the long run absolutely certain."[11]

Wow. How's that's for a hall-of-fame mystical narrative? Most of the remainder of *Cosmic Consciousness* consists of other accounts of mysticism that Bucke researched and compiled following his own experience, but he also offered his own thoughts as to what the mystical experience means to humanity as a whole. Some of these are of immense significance and we'll discuss them in greater detail later.

More Mystical Narratives and the Lessons Therein

It's worth starting here by saying there is now an enormous number of documented mystical experiences, a very large percentage of which were recorded starting early last century. Hundreds can be found on one website, imere.org, which is a great resource for people looking to examine these experiences in more depth. But for our purposes we'll highlight just a few, chosen for the variety of insights deriving from them.

If there is one quality that comes shining through most powerfully from the experience, it is the overwhelming joy and love the subjects feel. Sir Francis Younghusband was beholding the magnificence of the Himalayans when he said, "I had a curious sense of being literally in love with the world. I felt as if I could hardly contain myself for the love which was bursting within me. It seemed as if the world itself were nothing but love. . . . At

11. Bucke, *Cosmic*, 8–10.

the back and foundation of things I was certain was love—and not merely placid benevolence, but active, fervent, devoted love, and nothing less."[12]

Jim Harrison was a farmer in Zimbabwe and pilot who flew military missions during World War II. One day while sadly reflecting on his ill wife he questioned the reality of a God that seemed to be ignoring her prayers for healing, but then he had an insight that God was not to blame for her illness and loved her nonetheless. He then directed his own love toward God and felt "this love being passed on and on, and then suddenly it returned— a brilliant shaft of light from out of the sky . . . permeating me with such an intensity of happiness and love as to halt me in my tracks with a jump for joy. . . . So then I knew for certain God does indeed exist, that he is love, that he is joy, that he is light, that he stems from within as much as from without."[13]

These two examples are not more remarkable than hundreds of others that could have been selected, but beyond the love the subjects describe feeling, they also note the sense that God and creation are made of love and love itself is the power and substance of the universe. God is love indeed, just as the Bible tells us.

Another oft-described feature of the experience is how subjects feel themselves emerging from their sense of separate identity and entering into unity and oneness with all. Bernadette Roberts shared an interesting account of this happening to her on a camping trip in the Sierra Mountains. It started when she noticed a shift in visual perspective. "I soon noticed that when I visually focused in on a flower, an animal, another person, or any particular object, slowly the particularity would recede into a nebulous oneness, so that the object's distinctness was lost to my mind."[14] This sense became very acute on a trip to Big Sur when she watched a seagull fly by. "It was as if I was watching myself flying, for there was not the usual division between us. Yet, something more was there than just a lack of separateness, 'something' truly beautiful and unknowable . . . I thought to myself: for sure, this is what they mean when they say, 'God is everywhere.'"[15]

Raynor Johnson gave this account from an anonymous man who had an experience of oneness while sitting and waiting in a train station. He described it being a "commonplace scene," but "suddenly, I was aware of

12. Younghusband, *Heart*, 168.

13. Coxhead, *Relevance*, 43.

14. Roberts, *Experience*, 34.

15. Roberts, *Experience*, 30.

some mysterious current of force . . . which seemed to sweep through that small drab waiting room. I looked at the faces of those around me and they seemed to be suffused with an inner radiance. I experienced in that moment a sense of profoundest kinship with each and every person there. I loved them all! It was an all-embracing emotion, which bound us together indissolubly in a deep unity of being. I lost all sense of personal identity then. We were no longer separate individuals, each enclosed in his own private world. . . we were one with each other and with the Life which we all lived in common."[16]

It stands to reason these experiences of union and oneness would, if followed or carried out even more, lead ultimately to the unitive state with God, as described by Underhill and others. Fourteenth-century Catholic mystic Henry Suso described it this way. "When the spirit by the loss of its self-consciousness . . . is set free from every obstacle to union and . . . it passes away out of itself into God. . . . In this merging of itself in God the spirit passes away."[17] Similarly, Sufi mystic Al-Junayd said, "The saint . . . is submerged in the ocean by unity, by passing away from himself. . . . He leaves behind him his own feelings and actions as he passes into the life with God."[18]

Some mystics have told of an amazing expansion of their visual abilities which allowed them to see beyond normal and into the living spirit of what usually seems inanimate. Irina Starr was a twentieth-century spiritual writer from Los Angeles who described her experience in *The Sound of Light*. "Everything around me had come to life in some wonderous way and was lit from within with a moving, living, radiance. . . . I saw into them with an inner vision, and it was this inner sight which revealed the commonplace objects around me to be of the most breathtaking beauty . . . everything was literally alive; the light was living, pulsating, and in some way I could not quite grasp, intelligent. The true substance of all I could see was this living light, beautiful beyond words."[19] This sounds like the emanated Christ of Creation, as described in the gospel of John 1:1, immersing physical matter with life, light, and spirit.

The eternal now that Eckhart Tolle (among others) insists is the basis of reality is reported in other mystical accounts. Eighteenth-century French

---

16. Johnson, *Watcher*, 84.

17. Suso, *Life*, 307.

18. Stahl, *Most Surprising*, 87.

19. "Mystical Experience of Irina Starr."

mystic Madame Guyon said, "When my spirit had been enlightened . . . past, present, and future are there in the manner of a present and eternal moment, not as prophecy . . . but as everything is seen in the present in the eternal moment, in God himself."[20] Arthur Osborn wrote in *The Expansion of Awareness*, "Eternity exists at every moment on the time plane. It is Here Now just as much as at any future time."[21] Finally, no less than thirteenth-century German Meister Eckhart, who would be on the Mount Rushmore of Christian mystics if there was one, once said, "There [in eternity] you have in a present vision everything which ever happened or ever will happen. There is no before or after, there in eternity; everything is present and in this ever-present vision I possess everything."[22]

Something else mystics derive from their experience is the conviction that truth has been revealed to them, and they can with absolute certainty accept as objective knowledge that which they have learned through their perceptions. Once more we'll turn to William James. "Mystical experiences are as direct perceptions of fact for those who have them as any sensations ever were for us [non-mystics]."[23] Mystic and contemporary philosopher Ken Wilber wrote, "In the mystical consciousness, Reality is apprehended directly and immediately. . . subject and object become one in a timeless and spaceless act that is beyond any and all forms of mediation."[24] And because perhaps poets can convey this type of thing best, let's look at what the great Alfred Tennyson wrote in a letter to physicist John Tyndall: "By God Almighty! There is no delusion in the matter! It is no nebulous ecstasy, but a state of transcendent wonder, associated with absolute clearness of mind." In another letter Tennyson wrote, "Individuality itself seemed to dissolve and fade away into boundless being, and this not a confused state but the clearest, the surest of the surest—utterly beyond words, where death was an almost laughable impossibility, the loss of personality (if so it were) seeming no extinction, but the only true life."[25] And as it should go without saying, Tennyson's "death was an almost laughable impossibility" is an impression contained in virtually every mystical experience, correlating with other metaphysical realizations.

20. "Mystical Experience of Madame Guyon."

21. Osborn, *Expansion*, 244.

22. Fox, *Breakthrough*, 104.

23. James, *Varieties*, 415.

24. Wilber, *Quantum*, 5.

25. James, *Varieties*, 374–75.

A final lesson of the mystical experience we'll look at may be the most significant, because it shows what the future holds for humanity and is not indicative of a current condition, as glorious as those are. This is the one that tells us the ultimate destiny of human consciousness.

Spiritual Evolution: Where All This is Going

Mystics and some of the greatest intellects in history have said that just as all biological life on Earth has progressed through millions of years of the evolutionary process, human consciousness is evolving in the same way and will eventually be absorbed into the Divine. In other words, Homo sapiens in their entirety will attain something like the unitive life of the great mystics and perhaps even a state of divinization or theosis.

Spiritual evolution is hardly a new concept. It probably predates Darwinian evolution by more than twenty centuries, going back to the Eastern wisdom religions and Platonic thought well before the common era. After the rise of Christianity, it's been mostly limited to the Western esoteric traditions, but it had a significant resurgence after Darwin and the late nineteenth-century rise of theosophy and New Thought religion.

Yet it was Richard Maurice Bucke who was among the most influential in promulgating this concept. In his book *Cosmic Consciousness*, Bucke presented his belief that humanity is spiritually evolving every bit as much as physically evolving.[26] This means he believed that eventually all of humanity would progress from "self consciousness" (what we've mostly called ego-consciousness or ego-identity) to the cosmic consciousness he described experiencing in his narrative. He took the view that "our descendants will sooner or later reach, as a race, the condition of cosmic consciousness, just as, long ago, our ancestors passed from simple to self consciousness." This "would place the individual on a new plane of existence—would make him almost a member of a new species."[27] It's impossible to say what his intentions were in phrasing this point in this way, but it is amazing how it resembles what we know has happened in physical evolution. Life has evolved and changed one species into another.

Another tremendous contribution of Bucke was to show how cosmic consciousness is seen in the context of Christianity, especially in the example of the apostle Paul. "The Saviour of man is Cosmic Consciousness—in

26. Bucke, *Cosmic*, 3.

27. Bucke, *Cosmic*, 3.

Paul's language—the Christ."[28] That the words "cosmic consciousness" and "Christ consciousness" are often used interchangeably may have originated with Bucke. In his lengthy treatment of Paul, he makes a very compelling case that what happened to Paul on the road to Damascus was the onset of illumination or the unitive state, and that in virtually every instance when Paul used the words "Savior," "Christ," or "Christ Jesus," he was referring to cosmic consciousness.[29] He interpreted lengthy excerpts from the epistles in this way and showed how what Paul was expressing mirrors the way others have described what they learned from being in an advanced mystical state. One clear example is in 2 Cor 5:17, Paul wrote, "So if anyone is in Christ, there is a new creation: everything old has passed away; see, everything has become new!" (NRSV). Bucke also describes how when Paul referred to what could be considered the return or another coming of Christ, he really meant the time when all humanity advances into, or somehow receives, cosmic consciousness. "For as all die in Adam (self-consciousness), so all will be made alive in Christ (cosmic consciousness). But each in his own order: Christ the first fruits, then at his coming those who belong to Christ. Then comes the end when he hands over the kingdom to God the Father" (1 Cor 15:22–24 NRSV).

As stated before there are countless ways to do biblical exegesis, but Bucke was not a lonely outlier in this type of interpretation. Starting in the late nineteenth century this became common among the emerging metaphysical or New Thought churches, with Unity and Christian Science being examples. It is also applicable to much more than the Pauline Epistles. When much of the Bible is interpreted through the lens of evolving human consciousness, meanings become a lot clearer. The Garden of Eden story is a prime example.

When the mythical original humans ate the forbidden fruit they gained the knowledge of good and evil. This symbolizes humanity advancing from simple to self-consciousness, and humans for the first time conceived of themselves as individual entities distinct and separate from all else in the physical world. It also represents the birth of dualistic thought in human consciousness. And most ominously, this is when humanity first lived with the knowledge of their inevitable deaths. So, while this is considered an advance in consciousness, in most ways humans were much happier beforehand. Self-consciousness allowed humanity to make the proverbial

28. Bucke, *Cosmic*, 6.

29. Bucke, *Cosmic*, 113.

quantum leap in empirical knowledge, but at the cost of being trapped in a miserable psychological state. What can rescue us from this misery? What is our Savior? The coming of the Christ, or more precisely, the coming of Christ/cosmic consciousness, is the only thing that can end humanity's psychological estrangement with God and establish full conscious harmony and oneness with Divinity.

Yet despite how cogent this concept is for many of us, spiritual evolution remained a fringe theory in the Christian world through much of the twentieth century and is only slightly more accepted today. In all likelihood, one factor having a lot to do with this is the anti-science bias that mainstream Christianity is sadly known for. Most people in the church today have been indoctrinated into rejecting biological evolution for various reasons, as it is somehow seen as anti-God and an affront to biblical literalism. So, if biological evolution is verboten for these folks, spiritual evolution is further beyond the pale.

However, in the mid-twentieth century, an all-time great intellectual giant came upon the scene, and he advanced and legitimized the theory of spiritual evolution while virtually inventing the now ubiquitous field of science and religion. His name: Pierre Teilhard de Chardin.

Teilhard de Chardin (often referred to as just "Teilhard" in publication) was a Frenchman who lived in the first half of the twentieth century and was a Jesuit priest and paleontologist, an unusual vocational combination if there ever was one. He came to his Catholic faith early in life and was ordained a Jesuit priest in 1911 when he was thirty years old. Throughout his education he proved highly adept in the natural sciences, and shortly after his ordination he started working in a paleontology lab in France. His work in this field confirmed for him the truth of biological evolution, which when combined with his devout Catholic faith led to his groundbreaking theories blending science and religion in ways unheard of at the time.[30]

How dynamite was this guy? The Catholic Church, recognizing a challenge to its authority when it sees it, prohibited the publication of Teilhard's work during his lifetime.[31] As a result, none of his books, including the monumental *The Phenomenon of Man*, were published until his death in 1955, and not until 1959 in English.

It's impossible to do justice to Teilhardian theory in brief, and what follows may be more than a bit simplistic, but basically Teilhard believed

---

30. Grim and Tucker, "Biography."

31. Grim and Tucker, "Biography."

that evolution was the basis of all reality, which includes the physical and spiritual realms. One might even venture to say that Teilhard considered "evolution" much like Alfred North Whitehead considered "process," as an innate energy or force within creation which inexorably carries it forward. He also understood the spiritual realm as existing strictly within a Christian context, so like Bucke before him, he interpreted certain scriptural passages in a way that amounted to, for him, to be biblical validation of spiritual evolution. He, also like Bucke, was heavily influenced by the apostle Paul and the Pauline epistles. Finally, Teilhard theorized that the culmination or final destination that human consciousness would come to via spiritual evolution is what he called the Omega Point, which bears more than a passing resemblance to Bucke's cosmic/Christ consciousness.

This is not to even remotely suggest that Teilhard appropriated ideas or concepts from Bucke in any way. Teilhard spent nearly all his life in Europe and Asia, and it is unlikely that he'd even heard of Bucke, at least not before completing his most influential work. What if any similarities exist between the two says more about the concept of spiritual evolution than it does either person. That two obviously mammoth intellects can come to similar conclusions on a metaphysical theory despite considering substantially different evidence, in very different milieus, says a lot to substantiate spiritual evolution. The important thing both men had in common was that they were certified mystics. Being able to contemplate human consciousness from the mystical perspective probably had more to do with the conclusions they reached than anything else.

One Pauline verse that Teilhard was especially inspired by was 1 Cor 15:28: "When all things are subjected to him, then the Son himself will also be subjected to him who put all things in subjection under him, that God may be all in all" (ESV). There's a whole lot of subjection being discussed here, but Teilhard interpreted this to mean that "when all things are subjected to" the "Son," the Christ, was when all human consciousness would be completely absorbed into or replaced by Christ consciousness.[32] But a couple of other things about this are even more significant. First, Teilhard understood this Christ to be the incarnational Christ we discussed earlier, as seen in the creation story at the beginning of the gospel of John, or in another of his favorite Pauline verses, Col 1:15–17. "He is the image of the invisible God, the firstborn of all creation. For by him all things were created . . . all things were created through him and for him. And he is

32. Lyons, *Cosmic Christ*, 39.

before all things, and in him all things hold together" (ESV). Second, this spiritual evolution into Christ consciousness will precede when "God may be all in all," which is the end of history, or culmination of reality, that Teilhard referred to as the Omega Point, or as he described it, "the universe fulfilling itself in a synthesis of centres in perfect conformity with the laws of union. God, the Centre of centres. In that final vision the Christian dogma culminates. And so exactly, so perfectly does this coincide with the Omega Point."[33] This is when creation/the universe will ultimately be reunited with the Divine and will complete the process of apocatastasis that we described earlier.

Did Teilhard have critics or detractors? Bunches of them. But for this writer, Teilhard's critics can be lumped into the type that Claude Rains called "the usual suspects" in Casablanca. Criticism from the church was entirely predictable and based mostly on how his theories challenged Catholic authority and doctrine, such as original sin. Equally predictable is the criticism that's come from physicalist physics and science. These are the folks whose intellects are incapable of perceiving a reality that isn't physically determined in its entirety. They may think their perspective, which can be called scientism or physicalism, doesn't constitute a belief system, but it does, and it's every bit as dogmatic as any that can be seen in organized religion. From here, it's easy to visualize Teilhard coming to his convictions from a much higher perch, and a far greater view of reality, than any of his critics have ever reached.

33. Teilhard de Chardin, *Phenomenon*, 294.

Chapter 8

Traditional Spiritualities
Their Place in the New Faith

IN THE INTRODUCTION WE briefly considered how religion and spirituality have evolved throughout human history. We saw that because people conceived of their spirituality in two distinct ways, there's been a divergence in how it has been practiced. The religions that arose to facilitate these spiritualities could also be placed in two categories. Group One is comprised of those people who have felt compelled to seek the Divine within. Their instincts told them that the best or perhaps only way to comprehend the meaning of their existence was by examining their inner selves to see if they could discover the source of their being and All Being. Eventually this quest came into greater expression through the creation of the Eastern wisdom traditions, most prominently represented by Hinduism and Buddhism.

Group Two are those people who for some reason never felt or didn't pursue the instinctive need to search their inner selves to comprehend their existence and that of creation. They looked outwardly at and beyond creation and stretched their imaginations to find explanations for what they were and what they saw. Ultimately the great revelation-based traditions arose to provide some of the answers they were seeking.

And there you have it. We humans have always been a stubborn bunch when it comes to our metaphysics. But regardless, among those of us who have spent a large portion of their lives thinking about these things (OK, me), there is a desire to bring the faith in which we've grown up (Christianity) in a new direction. So, the time has come to think about what the

80

qualities of a new way of Christian faith can be and how people of both spiritual types can find their place and thrive in it.

First though it must be said that the need for a new, reformed faith is very real and becomes greater each day. Undoubtedly, mainstream Christianity does not offer the truth or spiritual well-being to its followers. How could it, considering the horrible theology that was made official church doctrine sixteen-odd centuries ago? I could continue to go down this rabbit hole and examine all that's gone wrong for Christianity since the rise of Roman Catholicism, but a lot of that ground has been covered already. Suffice it to say that any faith based on false, fabricated premises is doomed to obsolescence at some point.

In the meantime, just waiting for this obsolescence to arrive is no longer an option, if indeed it ever was. There are too many Christians right now who are in desperate need of a new way of Christian faith, even if they may not realize it. It's painful to even think about the people who have been spiritually misled and harmed by the church over the centuries. The resurgence of Christian Universalism the past two decades has been a fantastic development, but the time is nigh to take it to another level. The church has kept generations of Christians in a state of arrested spiritual development for far too long, and the sooner a reformed faith can come to their religious rescue, the sooner they can know what real spiritual fulfillment means.

An understandable question at this point is that if Christianity has gone this far off the rails, why try to reform it? Wouldn't it be smarter just to abandon it altogether? We believe the answer is no, and there are at least two significant reasons why. First, the Christianity that is now so deeply flawed is not the Christianity that was formed by the apostles and existed for centuries after Jesus, previously referred to here as Original Christianity. That faith was stolen from us by a power-seeking institution. Second, we also believe that despite the church's flaws, what we have encountered in the person of Jesus is an authentic experience of divinity. We can fully trust that what we heard in his words, seen by his actions, and learned from his teachings have given us insights into the spiritual realm that we would have never gotten otherwise. Finally, we think that Jesus would want us to reclaim the faith he originally bestowed to us.

The Four Stages of Spiritual Development

The phrase "arrested spiritual development" was used a few paragraphs ago, and it is not a mischaracterization of what has taken place in the church throughout history. Author M. Scott Peck described why this is the case in his book *Further Along the Road Less Travelled*, in which he presents what he considers to be the four stages of spiritual growth. By examining these stages, we can see how the existing church has failed us and why a reformed faith/church is so badly needed.

Peck's first stage is what he calls the chaotic/antisocial, and the people in it "are characterized by an absence of spirituality and are unprincipled."[1] It may be helpful to imagine people in this stage as having gone through childhood, adolescence, and reaching young adulthood without ever receiving any kind of religious or spiritual formation. They are living their lives adrift in a world without meaning or purpose, ethical awareness, or even a concept of divinity. Being in such a miserable state makes some of these people convert into stage two, known as the formal/institutional stage, in which "people depend upon the Church to govern their lives."[2] The church gives them the meaning, purpose, and stability they have so badly lacked. They have been given an understanding of God as Creator and the rules that must be followed to stay in God's good graces and go to heaven after their physical demise.

So far, so good, right? Well, yes, to a point. But this is also where a lot of problems start, and spiritual development begins to be restricted. The main problem is the church insists that for people to successfully follow their religion as it is presented to them, they must always stay in stage two. Spiritual growth is against the rules, and the rules can't even be questioned. If they don't think, believe or do precisely what the church tells them to, then they are violating what God has mandated for them and run the risk of eternal damnation.

In a very real way, the church relies on keeping its people in stage two spiritual captivity forever, and sadly, many of them become so intimidated and feel so trapped by the church they submit to it. And with the church wielding the ultimate punishment of eternal hell against its transgressors, it's understandable why submission seems a much wiser option to so many.

---

1. Peck, *Further Along*, as quoted in Fristad, *Destined*, 93.
2. Peck, *Further Along*, as quoted in Fristad, *Destined*, 93.

Stage three awaits those people who can summon the courage not to submit. They question the so-called truth that the church dominates them with and, instinctively I believe, begin to sense there must be something more to spiritual life. The thought that God, the creator of all and supposedly a loving one at that, would bestow life to billions of human beings only to toss the vast majority of them into eternal damnation becomes ridiculous and asinine to them, as it should. Peck calls this the skeptic/individual stage and those who reach it "are invariably truth seekers."[3] They begin to see reality in a larger, more wholistic way, far beyond the confines of what the church has forced upon them. They realize there is much more space for their spiritual consciousness to grow into, and much more spiritual truth for them to know.

Finally, as they follow upon these realizations further, they enter the mystical/communal stage, the fourth and final one. Here, people "are able to see the interconnectedness between all of life and God."[4] They can embrace life's mysteries and are excited to learn more about what they don't know. They are comfortable in their expanded reality. They're way past stage two, where people need every question about existence or aspect of reality rigidly answered and defined for them.

There are definite similarities between Peck's mystical/communal stage and what Evelyn Underhill called the awakening, the first of her five stages of mysticism. They could almost be equated or considered synonymous. For people at this level, "it finally dawns on our consciousness that there must be a better way to live; this world as we experience it does not live up to our expectations . . . there must be more to life . . . we are now ready for an awakening to a new reality, to consciousness of a divine Reality."[5] These are the people who are definitely ready and prepared to participate fully in our reformed faith/church as we are envisioning it.

And if you've detected a lot of similarity between Peck's formal/institutional stage two and what we've called Group Two spirituality, you've made an excellent observation. In both cases, the people are beholden to the spirituality that's been dictated to them. They've been indoctrinated into thinking it's the only "true" spirituality that exists, because it is derived from the only "true" religion that exists. These are the folks to which hopefully, as described earlier, "a reformed faith can come to their religious rescue."

3. Peck, *Further Along*, as quoted in Fristad, *Destined*, 93.

4. Peck, *Further Along*, as quoted in Fristad, *Destined*, 93.

5. Stahl, *Most Surprising*, 150.

Besides That, Mrs. Lincoln, How Did You Like the Play?

But on the other hand, it hasn't been all bad! Even with the overriding false narrative imposed upon the faithful and disguised as truth, many of those who could be described as being in Group Two or Peck's formal/institutional stage have, through heartfelt devotion to their faith, been able to experience genuine moral and spiritual formation. So, making the reformed faith/church we desire will not involve bulldozing the existing church first, and for that we are grateful. Perhaps a preliminary step in this effort would be to examine the church's strengths and consider what is essential in any Christian church.

If there is one quality prevalent in the church and Group Two spirituality that can go missing in Group One, it is the spiritualization of behavioral and relational life. The mainstream church has been successful in teaching that the will of God can be expressed, or not, through ethical behavior, interpersonal relations, and the basic doing of good deeds. For example, let's consider the many people in mainstream churches who have learned to accept God's grace, emulate the Christ, "die daily" in ego, and make selfless service to others a part of their lives. These admirable people, who give of themselves and do good works that benefit others, are ultimately rewarded for it. They may not be materially rewarded (not obviously anyway) but the spiritual gifts they receive more than compensates for whatever effort they put into their work. There's a saying I love that applies here: goodness is its own reward. The charitable person feels lighter, happier, more carefree. The time they spend doing good for others allows them to get out of their own heads for a while. They don't have to grapple with their egos, constantly searching for the next thought or pleasure that will give them a fleeting moment of contentment. The verse "whosoever will save his life shall lose it, and whosoever will lose his life for my sake shall find it" (Matt 16:25 NRSV) is as applicable here as when it described overcoming ego consciousness in an earlier chapter. In this instance the person losing their "life" is losing the constant need to pursue external gratification for their ego through more wealth, sex, or power. They then "find" the life of genuine soul satisfaction that comes through giving to something outside of yourself.

A quality related to this in the life of many mainstream churches is their commitment to the pursuit of social justice, in their communities and around the world. This almost as much as anything allows people to follow the teachings of Jesus and recreate his message and impact in the modern world.

These qualities highlight an absolutely essential feature for every Christian church, and that is its members are encouraged to perform good works. One of the ongoing debates in the Christian world, especially since the Protestant reformation, is what is most significant in Christian life: faith or good works? Sadly, in many churches today, having faith in Jesus as savior and vicarious atonement has made the need to perform good works almost irrelevant. If a new, reformed faith/church is going to be a significant improvement on what exists now, it must strongly emphasize Jas 2:17: "So you see, faith by itself isn't enough. Unless it produces good deeds, it is dead and useless" (NLT).

Bringing the Mystical Christ to "Saved" Christians

It is understandable why many modern Christians mistrust Group One spirituality. The ways in which their faith has been preached and taught to them has minimized the need or even discounted the possibility of the direct experience of God. Contemplation and meditation have been depicted as being almost exclusive practices of Eastern wisdom traditions and not needed by those who have accepted Jesus as their "savior." As a result, many people from these religious faiths just want to believe they're going to heaven when they die. Cultivating their souls or seeking a higher degree of spiritual wellness and understanding, even if it results in the greatest possible personal happiness, hardly seems worth the effort.

Another problem is that even among Christians who have interest in the mystical path, it seems too difficult, and they have a hard time believing that becoming enlightened is something God truly expects of us. Surely, the thinking is that there must be ways of faith that validate and redeem oneself in God's eyes that don't require undoing the effects of decades of entrenched, ego-induced thought patterns. Even if the common perception of reality is distorted by illusion, or what Hindus call Maya, that isn't our fault or something God blames us for. That is the result of humanity being victimized by a force it cannot control or overcome.

These beliefs should be understandable for any objective observer of the human condition. It is certainly easier for people, when faced with a situation that requires a moral choice to be made, to intentionally direct their minds to make the "right" decision or take the "right" action. Not that it's a slam dunk. The ego, being what it is, will do what it can to make the person choose to do what benefits the ego-identity. But a person who has been instructed by their faith that there is a higher ideal or a greater good to be attained in the sight of God by making more self-sacrificing choices will often do so. And they are able to do so because God's grace, freely given to all without merit, inspires them to give lovingly as God has given to them.

There are also some people who question what type of good results from contemplative or meditative practices, and that's understandable too. From a certain vantage point, it can appear that spending a lot of time meditating doesn't benefit anyone besides the practitioner. Now, from a broader, more erudite perspective on spirituality, there is the certainty that isn't true. Aspirants who attain enlightenment actually perform a tremendous service for their loved ones and all of humanity. When mystical realization is attained it elevates the consciousness of everyone in that mystic's orbit and may even hasten humanity's progress in its continuing spiritual evolution. Mystics are also instilled with devout love for their fellow humans and compelled to serve them as they are best able. Yet, it's easy to see how our Group Two friends can see meditation as being a somewhat selfish practice, or why people may feel it's a greater good to volunteer in a soup kitchen or take part in other charitable activities. There are clearly "others" who benefit from that type of "selfless" action. It's the very definition of altruism.

So, when introducing people to the mystical Christ, there must be an understanding that it is something that many will find difficult or even intimidating. Even the sincerest people, who understand that attaining mystical consciousness is the true purpose of human existence, can wonder if there is another level of spiritual achievement that at least allows for the conviction that one is attuned to and in harmony with the divine will for their lives. Is there another plateau of religious life that, while not as high as the one the great mystics or ascended masters reach, still provides the peace and contentment that can be understood as coming from God?

People shouldn't feel that they have failed in their religious lives if they don't eventually become fully enlightened or attain Christ consciousness. Your humble writer certainly doesn't want to feel that way. This book is not being authored in some invisible spiritual realm by an ascended being. So, I know as well as anybody it's important for people not to be too hard on themselves. Believe me, there's plenty of reasons why there's only been one guy we know of who was able to walk on water, even if that same person said that if we followed him, we'd be able to do all that he did and more.

No one is excluded from divine love and God wants us to have a palatable sense of that. That's really what Christian Universalism is all about. So, a new, reformed faith needs to create that impression as well. Joyful, loving, and spiritually nourishing communion with God is not reserved just for those on the Top 1,000 Holiest People of All Time list. We are not being held to a standard of spiritual achievement reached by just a rare few before we can perceive at least a measure of God's grace.

If there is a gentle and effective way to introduce the mystical Christ to people, it may be to teach the ways in which their happiness is affected by not having a Group One dimension in their spirituality. They'll still have that vague feeling of alienation that results when the ego makes its inevitable return to dominance in their consciousness, no matter how much altruism they practice. They will feel there's a psychic wall of separation between them and God and all of creation. As much as they may love those dear to them, making a real soul-to-soul connection isn't possible. There's a constant onslaught of involuntary thought that they are unable to control and denies them inner peace. The material world around them, even the natural world, seems to be soulless matter untouched by the sacred or divine. Most significantly, the God of their being and all being, no matter how devoutly they believe in it, only exists in an abstract realm that's forever out of their reach, or at least as long as they live. A direct, personally transformative experience of God is out of the question. They feel pretty much destined to live the rest of their lives feeling just like they do now, worn out, plagued by doubt and concerns, with only brief, intermittent moments of ego contentment to relieve their constant, suffocating malaise.

It is vitally important and perhaps essential to the ultimate success of our reformed faith that mainstream Christians come to trust Group One spirituality and understand what the mystical Christ means and represents. They must know that they can devote themselves to a new way of Christian faith, tremendously enrich their lives, and still retain all the spiritual virtues they have gotten from their mainstream church.

Group One, Don't Be Smug

Group One spirituality also has issues that hopefully our reformed faith will be able to address. First, many from Group One are often solely focused on the interior/experiential aspect of religious life, and the behavioral/relational is not as important. Social justice and good works are often seen as peripheral. It's not because they don't think there needs to be a greater force for good in the world or there aren't moral or ethical standards worth having. But there is among some a belief that these morals, ethics, and desire to do good will arise naturally in the aspirant through continued devotion to interior/experiential spirituality. Of course, this could very well be a practical truism, although I don't think there is an organic cause and effect to it, at least before mystical realization is attained.

There also in Group One can be an attitude of skepticism or even disdain towards the objective world they see before their eyes, as opposed to what they experience between their ears. Even if they can conceive that there is a quality of the Divine underlying all nature, they fail to recognize its spiritual significance. They may even think the behavioral/relational part of their lives is totally irrelevant to their spiritual aspirations.

This perspective, however, carries with it some significant risk. The mystical path can be a lonely road to travel. Most of us who have been led to take this journey are lifelong "seekers," who have instinctively known there was more to human life than meets the eye. Then, after reading copious amounts of religious literature, both classic and contemporary, we discover our instincts were correct. There is a spiritual and transcendent purpose to our existence, and it is in making the conscious realization of our soul's eternal oneness with God. Upon attaining this state of consciousness, the fullness of joy and happiness available to each human being is experienced. Just acquiring the objective knowledge of this mystical reality is a joyous, life-changing event. It gives people the meaning and purpose they've been seeking. However, the first thing one learns afterwards is that knowing about it and consciously experiencing it are two entirely different things. Having that knowledge is first edifying, even exhilarating, but soon the euphoria fades and is replaced by a sense of self-doubt. Your everyday mindset, which you may have been reasonably comfortable with, is suddenly inadequate. You feel challenged to make changes in how you use your mind and may have been led to believe that meditation is the only possible way to achieve success.

Anything that points people in the right spiritual direction is of course a positive thing. For many people though, the quest to embark on the mystical path presents challenges they never knew existed. Practicing mindfulness and presence is not like practicing the guitar. It's all in the mind, and the ego therein can put up some stiff resistance. It can be hard just to get started. Then suddenly, just engaging in your everyday simple pleasures or distractions, like watching a movie or a ball game, comes with twinges of guilt. An inability to be mindful while doing housework is frustrating.

Thoughts of tomorrow's pedicure while you are watching a sunset are a major annoyance. What you think was a "bad" meditation session makes you feel discouraged or defeated.

Eventually, you get a sense that there's a battle going on in your head between your soul and your mind. The new you wants to uncover and enhance your soul consciousness through your spiritual practice, but your ego-identity keeps interfering, telling you to goof off on social media and relax. You start to get nagging feelings that whatever you're doing at any given time would be better spent doing something more God-worthy. That's when you realize you have it. You have the spirit monkey on your back.

As onerous as all this sounds, though, there is a simple explanation for it. First, the most likely reason people have these feelings is that they've put all their spiritual eggs in one religious basket. They have, upon discovering that the mystical experience is a real, actual thing, started believing nothing short of full-blown spiritual enlightenment gives a person any sense of soul satisfaction, and meditation alone is the only way to get there. So, they put a huge amount of pressure on themselves. They may even, depending on how old they are, think they only have X number of years left to reach the spiritual heights of Yogananda or St. John of the Cross. It doesn't make for a serene or productive religious practice. Then there is the fact that even the most devout practitioners seldom meditate for more than an hour each day. That leaves twenty-three hours for them to curse their ego, think they are disappointing God, and feel they're wasting their lives.

And this is because many of them won't see or consider the presence of the Divine that is saturating the landscape right in front of them. They can't fathom the ways of sacred interaction or communion with the Divine that exist in every waking moment, especially in those moments with fellow humans. In short, they don't understand the spiritual well-being that can be found in some of the everyday things, away from the meditation mat, that many Group Two folks do.

Yes, it is true that interior, meditative spirituality is the most direct and intentional way of mystical realization. But surely all of history's great mystics also spiritualized and made sacred their exterior lives as well. They recognized the divinity of creation and in the souls of their human family. It's even possible that they had a breakthrough in their relational life before there was a corresponding one in their meditative experience. The important thing is not the sequence of events, but just knowing that holiness applies to every aspect of life, with each supporting and strengthening the other. No one who has ever attained mystical consciousness has ever, when getting off their mat or blanket and emerging from their home, lived among others in the outside world in an egocentric, amoral way. Another way of putting it is that St. Paul, upon finishing one of his epistles to the Corinthians, didn't mosey on over to the apostolic lounge for happy hour and start hitting on the single ladies there. I feel very confident in stating that.

What this means is that many people who are more mystically or meditatively inclined would benefit greatly from having some good, old-fashioned faith instilled in them. Regardless of where they stand on the mystical path, they are still a child of God, unconditionally immersed in divine love. They can pray and still feel the Divine presence in their lives. When they love as God loves them, and selflessly give when they can, they will feel their relationship with God grow stronger. Basically, religious life is not the all or nothing thing they may have imagined it was. There are, short of transformative mystical realization, ways in which one can feel real spiritual well-being and the loving presence of the Divine.

Where does all this leave us? Hopefully, we've established that there is a vital need for a new way of Christian faith, and it can have faith elements in it that will allow people of every religious sensibility and spiritual inclination to thrive. The job now is to finally present what this new way of faith will be. This is when the hard work really begins.

Chapter 9

What We Believe
A New Way Forward for Our Faith

"But seek ye first the kingdom of God, and his righteousness; and all
these things shall be added unto you."

(MATT 6:33 KJV)

"Do not be conformed to this world but be transformed by the
renewing of your minds, so that you may discern what is the will of
God—what is good and acceptable and perfect."

(ROM 12:2 NRSV)

"That to achieve this unitive knowledge of the Godhead is the final
end and purpose of human existence."

(ALDOUS HUXLEY)[1]

WELL, HERE IT IS, from three unimpeachable sources. I believe when Jesus,
Paul, and Huxley tell you the path you should take in life, the ultimate goal
you should pursue, and the purpose of human existence, you should take
what they say as, well, gospel.

What does that mean for us now as we take this final part of our journey together? In basic terms, we need to reformulate all that we've discussed
so far so that, going forward, we can follow that path, pursue that ultimate

1. Bridgeman, *Huxley*, 13.

goal, and strive for that divinely ordained purpose of human existence, in a logical and methodical way. In other words, it's time to reveal the "new way of Christian faith" the previous chapter was hinting at.

What this will not be is a systematic theology. Allow me to recommend Paul Tillich if that's what you were hoping to see. Nor should this be considered a new/reformed faith or a new/reformed church, even if that terminology was used earlier. What is envisioned is a new way of faith that would fit snugly inside modern Christian Universalism, and that it also be something that can be practiced either within or independent of church affiliation or setting. Of course, as a CU minister, I would strongly encourage becoming part of a CU church if you are motivated and able to do so. There is no doubt that fellowship and companionship is hugely beneficial for anyone pursuing spiritual growth. Being part of a faith community can be very rewarding and practicing religion in isolation is very difficult. The Christian Universalist Association (CUA) is a wonderfully supportive organization for like-minded people, and churchgoers who adopt this new way of faith could find a welcoming home in any CU church. However, my hope is that this work and the ideas it presents will appeal to the general spiritual reader and people throughout the religious spectrum, even those who aren't inclined to affiliate with churches or denominations. So, as we proceed, ways in which this faith can be practiced individually and in a theoretical church setting will be described. However people live their religious lives, the hope is that if they are inspired by what they learn here and get a sense of cogency and truthfulness from it, they are able to apply it to their spirituality in the way most beneficial to them.

Of course, our new way needs to be called something, if only so those of you who adopt it can describe it to your friends. The problem is if naming things was a strength, a spiritual practice we discussed earlier wouldn't be called "never take life for granted." In the plainest language possible, it would best be called Christian Universalism with an added point of emphasis, but that clearly wouldn't work. So here goes. Ladies and gentlemen, now presenting, Mystical Christian Universalism (MCU).

As befitting its new name, MCU will strongly emphasize the mystical Christ and be rooted in Christian Universalism. And really, the only meaningful distinction between CU and MCU will be the latter's emphasis on the attainment of mystical realization/Christ consciousness being humanity's ultimate spiritual objective.

The first thing that needs to be established is why in MCU we believe so much in the primacy of mystical experience. And to do that we have to start by explaining the basic assumptions (BAs) we are starting our faith journeys with. BAs are the set of metaphysical concepts relating to spiritual matters we consider logically established, or the accepted knowledge on a spiritual subject matter that we take for granted. From these we determine the spiritual qualities we don't have full realization of, and thus the goals and objectives we must strive to attain.

We call BAs that apply to the spiritual dimension of human life "soul-views" to distinguish them from another type of BA we'll describe later, and some of them are as follows:

1. All life, including our life and that which animates every organism, is already eternal. We don't have to do or believe anything to gain or earn eternal life because we already have it.

2. Our lives are eternal because we are children of God in the truest sense. We are emanations of God and one with God in spirit, and this spirit is our true, essential identity.

3. We retain this spiritual identity when our lives in our current incarnations end. We are ultimately destined for greater experiences of life because we'll express more of our spiritual essence as we proceed through our eternal journeys.

4. Human life and all forms of life are of God, and it manifests and is experienced as consciousness. And just as the physical world and all things visible are processing and evolving, so too is it spiritually evolving, inevitably leading humanity to an advanced consciousness of its oneness with God. Christ consciousness, as it (among other things) has been called.

A fair question that some may have regarding these tenets is why we consider them BAs and not articles of faith or things we believe, and the plain answer is that for practical purposes it doesn't matter what we call them. Once they're accepted into our hearts and minds they are assumed to be true, and that's basically it. As for why are we so confident we can accept these tenets as established truths, I believe that answer can be found in the preceding eight chapters of this work, as well as in the Christian Universalist Association's list of "Our Beliefs," one of which states, "We believe that God's Holy Spirit has inspired numerous prophets, saints, philosophers, and *mystics* throughout history, in a variety of cultures and traditions; and that by reading the Bible (the authoritative textual basis of our faith) and other great texts of spiritual and moral wisdom with a discerning mind, and meditating to connect to the Spirit within, we may all gain a greater understanding of truth, which should be applied for the betterment of ourselves and our world."[2]

We believe that through the sources described in this faith statement, we have come to a "greater understanding of" metaphysical truths like those in the BAs listed above and in more we'll see later. We are particularly inspired by the wisdom and knowledge given us by mystical sources, as described in this book and elsewhere, and also accept it as truthful. Specifically, a critical point guiding us in the formation of MCU can be seen in tenet number one, and that is we don't have to do, believe, or achieve anything to manifest the spiritual qualities it describes that we have in our lives. They just are, through divine providence.

So, with these truths in mind, we are led to further consider what the overriding purpose of religious life should be. If we know we already have eternal life and are truly children of God, spiritual beings destined for greater experiences of existence after our current incarnations end, what is left for us to accomplish in our lives? The inescapable conclusion we have been led to is we must pursue the fully conscious realization of this knowledge, and in reaching this conclusion we experience what Underhill called our awakening. We now know that what we only hold in our empirical/intellectual thought we must experience in our souls, and this only occurs through the mystical experience. This is truly what God put us on earth to do. This is the heaven on earth we will strive for, not the heaven of the other church that you have to earn your way to before and for when you die. Ours is the kingdom of God of which Jesus spoke, the divine union described by the mystics, the cosmic consciousness of Bucke, the unitive state of Underhill, and so on. This will transform us (as Paul asked of us in Rom 12:2) into entirely new beings who are not what we thought we previously were. This is the heaven on earth that God wants us to attain in our lives right here, right now. The afterlife has nothing to do with it.

Another way to think of it is that being religious requires a person to do or believe something to satisfy God's will or intention for their life. In mainstream Christianity followers are asked to believe that God appointed Jesus to be a blood sacrifice to atone for humanity's sins. In MCU, we are

2. "Our Beliefs."

just asked to make an honest effort to transform our consciousness in a way that reveals the omnipresence of God and our essential oneness with God at the soul level. Why does God want this for us? With each mystical realization of this divine reality, we are cooperating and cocreating with God and helping to fulfill the divine plan God has in place to fully restore humanity to perfection through Christ and reunite it with its Source and Creator.

Other Basic Assumptions and MCU doctrine

There are other BAs we hold in MCU, and those pertaining to cosmology or creation are called "worldviews." Worldviews, along with our soulviews, act as a spiritual foundation and lead us to the creation of MCU doctrines like that we just described. Worldview is to universal being as soulview is to human and personal being.

An important thing to keep in mind about BAs is that they are not *what* we see or derive from our personal experience. BAs are the perspective, the *how* and *from what* we see. For example, our soulviews being as we've described them dictate we see everyone else the same way. This means that because we understand ourselves as children of God, spiritual beings one with God in essence and identity, we must look beyond the personality and physical facade we first encounter in others and see them with the same spiritual qualities we possess. A saying used among people in certain religious settings conveys this idea beautifully and it goes "the Christ in me sees and recognizes the Christ in you." It affirms the spiritual identity of those involved and elevates the interaction to a higher level.

In the same way, worldview is how we view and experience every other aspect of reality besides the personal and interpersonal. Our worldview is not what we deduce from observing the universe. It is the *how* we observe it, the perspective we observe it from.

Specifically, in our worldview, universe/creation is panentheistic in origin and in nature. Also, universe/creation is in the process of apocatastasis, meaning it is returning to the Divine Source from which it originally emanated at the beginning of time. You may recall we called it PanApoc. By assuming the reality of PanApoc, we can attribute several other characteristics to universe/creation that contribute to our worldview. Some of these are:

1. Divinity is the Source and Substance of All Being, and creation was the result of God's emanation of God's material component. Matter and Spirit have never been separate and have eternally coexisted with and as God. In the Trinitarian tradition, Creator God transcends creation, Christ is the divine emanation of creation, and Spirit unifies and permeates Creation.

2. As consciousness is a unique and inevitable expression of God, it is the preexistent basis for creation and pervades all its physical forms. As such, creation's material component derives from consciousness, not vice versa. This all-pervasive consciousness is an animating energy within all matter, as described in process theology and as the principle of panpsychism.

3. Assuming numbers 1 and 2, the universe can be considered conscious, alive, and intelligent, and as it is of God, loving, benevolent and purposeful.

4. Assuming numbers 1 and 2, the physical, material, visible manifestations of reality derive from a spiritual, immaterial, invisible, and conscious realm.

5. Through PanApoc, the meaning, direction, and purpose of the universe is revealed and understood. Universe/creation is evolving, spiritually and physically, and will inevitably be perfected through Christ and reunited with the Divine Source.

This final worldview, along with soulview number four, are of particular significance because when combined they create another doctrine of MCU, one that defines our teleology for both humanity and creation.

There is a powerful and beautiful correlation between humanity and creation. While creation is on the PanApoc journey, humanity cooperates with God and contributes to the divine plan through the spiritual evolution process as described by Teilhard. In other words, the road to Christ consciousness humanity is on is an integral part of the journey of apocatastasis all creation is on. Humanity can be considered as the crew and passengers of the good ship Creation (and perhaps somewhere in the deep recesses of space there are others), and the more we hasten our spiritual evolution through mystical realization, the more we accelerate ourselves toward the collective Christ consciousness of our destiny (as described by Bucke), and creation towards its final reunification with its Divine Source.

In the meantime, and on an individual basis, it is the attainment of Christ consciousness that is our salvation and Savior. Not in the sense that it is the only thing that keeps our souls from being extinguished or cast into some Dante-like hellscape, but because it ends our conscious estrangement, and establishes our full conscious harmony, with God. So, this is why MCU considers this our primary spiritual objective.

Not That It's Easy, or Fasten Your Seat Belts

It would be nice if being a devout MCU-er was as easy as believing in some convoluted and ridiculous doctrine, but authentic spiritual growth is not that simple. Aspirants will have to commit to some daily practices if they are to truly follow this path.

First and foremost, you guessed it, is daily meditation. All the great world religions have meditation traditions or schools of mysticism that are unique to them. In Judaism the prominent school of mysticism is called Kabbalah, in Islam it is known as Sufism. There are numerous Hindu practices, including all the various forms of yoga and Ramana Maharshi's self-inquiry. Buddhism is probably the most meditation-focused of all the world religions. It only exists because the Buddha himself vowed he would sit meditating under the bodhi tree until he reached enlightenment.

There are, of course, many Christian practices as well, and time-honored ones at that. Most of them came from the medieval monastic traditions of Roman Catholicism and the Eastern Orthodox Church and have been practiced for centuries. The Eastern Orthodox mystical school or tradition is called Hesychasm, and one of its main practices is the repetition and contemplation of the Jesus Prayer, which states "Lord Jesus Christ, son of God, have mercy on me, the sinner."[3] In Catholicism, the practice of Lectio Divina dates back to the third century and may have originated, ironically enough, with Origen, who was one of the original Universalists whose writings were declared anathema by Rome.[4] Lectio Divina is based on the belief that the Logos or Christ is alive in Scripture and that by meditating on certain passages the experience of the Christ within becomes tangible. The practice of apophatic theology became known through the fourteenth century classic of Christian mysticism *The Cloud of Unknowing*, which teaches the way of coming to an ascertainment of God through negation, or by contemplating

3. "Jesus Prayer."
4. Manneh, "Lectio Divina."

what the qualities of the Divine cannot be.[5] Yet as far as direct instruction from Jesus on prayer or meditation, there's not a lot besides what was in the Sermon on the Mount in Matt 6:6, "but when you pray, go away by yourself, shut the door behind you, and pray to your Father in private. Then your Father, who sees everything, will reward you" (NLT), shortly before he gave us the Lord's Prayer. In Ps 4:4 a similar idea is expressed: "When you are in your beds, search your hearts and be silent" (NRSV).

However, when we consider all the schools of mysticism and meditative practices of the world religions, it's most important to understand that mysticism is a universal ideal, one that is common and accessible to every human being regardless of religious background. So, in MCU, we believe the best meditation practice is the one that works best for the person doing it. Christians, Hindus, Buddhists, and people from no religious tradition have attained mystical realization, and virtually none of them (except maybe Ramana Maharshi, who seemed to be a persnickety sort) would insist one must be of their religion, or that their method or path, is the only way to be successful. True mystics have said with virtual unanimity that the experience transcends any attempt to label it as belonging to any single religion.

Let's recall the first thing aspirants must try to accomplish when starting their meditation practice. The most important thing is to regain control of our conscious thought away from our ego identities. We've all lost our minds, and by meditating we start to gain them back. We begin to resist the relentless train of unwanted thought the ego throws at us to trick us into identifying with it. We retake the wheel of our minds back from the ego-identity that runs our lives and regain the ability to think intentionally again. And when we do, we start to regain awareness of our souls, our true identities, underneath all the mental clutter that's been obscuring them.

In MCU, we believe it all starts with mindfulness. When we have cultivated the ability to fully engage in the present moment and occupy our consciousness in the here and now, that is when the battle begins to be won. And when aspirants become somewhat skilled in mindfulness and can practice it daily, both in meditation and going about their daily activities, they will instinctively know what other ways of meditation would work best for them, or if they even want to try another way. Consistency, much more than type, is the real key. Any technique that can be practiced every day without struggle is more important than the technique itself.

5. Johnston, *Cloud*, 8.

Get Thee Out of Doors and Adore God's Handiwork

As we know how often mystical experience results from the worship and contemplation of nature, we believe that MCU spiritual practice should also include daily meditation in the great outdoors. Again, this makes perfect sense, because God is revealed in panentheistic creation just as much as when we turn inward to find the divine nature of our souls. All is in and of God, and God is in all. We always have an opportunity to discover the Divine, whether we are directing our attention inwardly or outwardly.

At first, this can be a commitment to just spending a half hour a day outdoors, and I say this admitting that if I'm not paying attention, days at a time can go by and I'm not outdoors that much, especially in winter. For many people it takes intention. We just can't assume we're outdoors that length of time in the normal course of our lives, and by outdoors we don't mean driving from indoor space to indoor space. We mean being outdoors just for that purpose. And this isn't just for those of you who live in California. Even when the weather is less than ideal, we'll say that it is virtually never bad enough that this practice can't be kept.

If there's one thing I hope we have near unanimous agreement on, it is that just being outdoors is inspiring and rejuvenating to the spirit. When we're not closed in and surrounded by manufactured materials, our spirits expand and respond in a positive way, even if we're not immediately aware of it. We instinctively realize that we're in an environment that's greater than all of us and humanity isn't responsible for.

It's always good to get some biblical inspiration for something we should be doing, so let's consider a few verses on the subject. Job 12:7–10 states the case plainly. "But ask the animals, and they will teach you, or the birds in the sky, and they will tell you, or speak to the earth, and it will teach you, or let the fish in the sea inform you. Which of all these does not know that the hand of the Lord has done this? In his hand is the life of every creature and the breath of all mankind" (CEB). This is so obvious it hardly needs elucidation, but clearly these verses tell us that if we look at the natural world objectively, with a fresh perspective, we'll sense an unseen energy that is the power and foundation supporting all of it. We don't even have to discern it ourselves. The animals, birds, fish, and all the earth will speak the truth to us.

As you may imagine the wisdom books of the Hebrew Bible such as Psalms and Proverbs are filled with similar entreaties, with Ps 19:1 succinctly stating, "The heavens declare the glory of God, the skies proclaim the work of his hands" (CEB). They are not as prevalent in the New Testament, but Paul chipped in a noteworthy one in Rom 1:20, writing, "For since the creation of the world God's invisible qualities—his eternal power and divine nature—have been clearly seen, being understood from what has been made, so that people are without excuse" (CEB). Isn't that closing phrase great? It's like Paul saying you're a knucklehead if you can't see these things yourself.

Of course, what's most meaningful to every Christian is what Jesus had to say on a certain topic, and what he said about this are among his most widely known words in all the Gospels. Matthew 6:25–34 is the section of the Sermon on the Mount which contains his lesson on the lilies of the field, and in it Jesus implored his followers to look to nature and see the obvious ways God takes care of the entire natural world, implying that if it weren't for God's grace permeating all of nature none of it would survive or even exist. Jesus then allowed that bit of wisdom to lead to his greatest teaching of all. Do not worry about food, clothing, or shelter, because God knows you need those things and will provide them. Instead, humanity needs to make a new first priority for itself. In Matt 6:33 he said simply, "Seek ye first his kingdom, and his righteousness; and all these things shall be added unto you" (ASV).

Jesus did not say that seeing and realizing the Divine presence as the power permeating and supporting the natural world leads *directly* into the kingdom of God, just that the evidence of the Divine in nature should point in the direction of the kingdom of God. But combined with the other virtues of nature contemplation we've discussed, we trust there is an understanding of why in MCU we consider it a vital, essential feature of our spirituality.

So, how do we do this? It's trickier than saying we must practice traditional interior meditation or seek the Christ within. There are numerous methods of that, as well as plenty of guidance and instruction on how to practice them. Nature contemplation is not as well defined. Plus, as we have seen in some earlier examples, some mystical experiences occurring in nature were seemingly of the "out of the blue" variety, with the subject not necessarily pursuing them. Yet we also know that in some of these cases the subject was reverently experiencing their environment and spiritually discerning its divine qualities, even if they weren't realizing it.

One helpful thing the nature mystics have taught us is when we are observing any scene or event in the natural world we should try to project our perspective out of our sense of personal being. In other words, that bird you are watching make a nest would be doing this regardless of if you were watching her at all, or even if you existed at all. Watch intently, as if you are part of what you're seeing. You may feel yourself being cast into the oneness, the great unified existence, and know you are part of something much greater than your captive, solitary ego.

Some other good techniques were described earlier. In beginner's mind we do our best to reengage with the natural world as if for the first time. We forget what we think we know about nature and discover a renewed sense of wonder of it all. We are awe inspired by what we see and emerge out from under the conscious confines of our ego identities. We realize our egos play just a tiny role in the grand scheme of things, but our real selves are one with the abundant spirit of creation. We gain a palatable sense of the unseen power that is the source and sustenance of everything, including that flock of birds in the sky flying in a perfect V-formation toward warmer climes.

Never take life for granted works much the same way, but it is more a mental exercise than a sensory one. It asks us to reflect on all creation and humanity's place in it, not our immediate environment at a specific moment. But it still helps cultivate a feeling of enchantment in us, a sense that there must be something beyond comprehension that enables creation to be precisely as it is. Don't pretend some of the more spectacular features of the universe aren't important in your life or worth thinking about. No, they won't help you figure out how to fix your leaky faucet, but they are responsible for you and your faucet being here at all.

Maybe I'm the easily awestruck type, but I'm still intrigued as to why the world we live in is shaped like a sphere. I suppose it could have been flat, but a flat surface floating through space doesn't make any more sense than a sphere doing the same thing. It would explain though why people don't fall off it, unlike those of us on the bottom half of a sphere. And how did the planet form at all, regardless of shape, and why does it rotate on its axis and go in a circle around that bright thing in the sky? And why is the bright thing precisely the right size and distance away so that our existence is possible in the first place?

Hopefully this idea has been effectively conveyed, and the more one can learn about the universe and natural world the easier this practice becomes. It should help us understand that the power behind and through all being is far greater than any problem the "real world" can throw at us.

We Like the "Straw Gospel"

We also understand that our religious lives can't consist of meditation alone, whether indoors or outdoors. It must also include what we call the good works/love in action component, where we give of ourselves to benefit something outside of ourselves, without expectation of return. When we act in ways that don't serve our self-interest, we "empty our vessels" of self-centeredness, our ego identities diminish, and our divine nature begins to emerge.

This philosophy of the value of good works may be most identified in the New Testament with the book of James, which is why in MCU we hold James in such high regard. We believe its message greatly enhances our spiritual lives. But as an added bonus, we love James because it annoyed Martin Luther so much he called it the "epistle of straw" and wanted it removed from the Bible.[6] Why? Luther, the father of the Protestant Reformation, wanted Christian doctrine to be that faith in the church's narrative is the only thing required of us to win our salvation, and being a source of goodness in the world has nothing to do with it. Also, the faith that Luther prescribed had nothing to do with taking to heart Jesus's words, actions, or teachings. It was just about believing the original sin/vicarious atonement fairy tale Rome dreamed up about 1200 years before. Luther surely thought he was doing Christianity a big favor by rebelling against Roman Catholicism, but he didn't do anything to improve it. In fact, we're still dealing with Luther's influence over five centuries later. Far too many people believe they're good Christians because of their stated belief in Jesus as savior, while their actions reflect vehement opposition to Jesus's teachings and example.

This is not to belabor what's been said before about Christian orthodoxy, but to highlight why MCU considers good works/love in action as essential to our spirituality. One more time we'll let Jas 2:17 state it for us. "So you see, faith by itself isn't enough. Unless it produces good deeds, it is dead and useless" (NLT). An underlying message we see in this verse is that faith and goodness are interrelated, with each supporting the other. Doing good for others enriches our faith and makes it stronger, because it dilutes the power of self-interest and ego-identity in our minds and reveals more of the Divine within as the essence of our being. And faith without good works is "dead and useless" because it doesn't connect us to our spiritual selves in any meaningful way. Faith is reduced to assenting to a historical

6. "Letter of James."

statement in our thoughts, and it doesn't do anything to diminish the self-centeredness controlling our minds and concealing our souls.

Goodness is important in spirituality for many reasons. One is, as much as we emphasize coming to an experience of divinity through mysticism, pursuing that goal can be frustrating and feel unrewarding. Genuine impressions of personal spiritual growth can be elusive, and like with a lot of things, such as a new exercise program or healthier diet, when one can't feel healthier and happier right away their motivation to continue a practice can start to wane.

This is where being what everyone considers a good person comes in, and it's really pretty simple. It even sounds trite to describe it. I can imagine how it would sound to people if they heard someone say their new religious faith asks them to do good deeds every day. I'd probably chuckle a bit myself. But this simple thing is based on deep spiritual principles and is sure to bring positive results. When you selflessly act in another's best interest without expecting something for yourself in return, you give your ego-identity a real kick in its butt. It isn't used to not having near total control over you, and not dictating to you what you must do or think next to gratify it. You've wounded your ego, and with each good deed you do its power over you starts to fade, and you feel freer and happier as a result.

Not only that, but there's a deep satisfaction that comes with the conviction you are pleasing and obeying God, and by helping others that's exactly what you're doing. God is the "other," the person or persons you may never see or meet, because as Jesus said in Matt 25:40, "The King will reply, 'Truly I tell you, whatever you did for one of the least of these brothers and sisters of mine, you did for me'" (NIV). It doesn't have to be a grand, magnanimous gesture every day, though it's fair to say there are degrees of good deed doing too. It's good to pass a space in a parking lot so the person behind you can have it but shoveling the snow off an older neighbor's walkway is even better. There's not always an exact correlation between the effort required on your part and the degree of good you're doing, but the greater your effort the better you'll feel about yourself for making it.

The only other thing to add here is that this is something churches have always been great at. Most of them offer opportunities to participate in larger-scale charitable endeavors that are farther reaching and have greater impact. So, by all means keep doing good for others through your personal spiritual practice but also consider looking into how local churches can magnify your goodness and be a greater blessing in the world.

Thou Shalt Not What?

However, as we have all seen, Christianity has unfortunately always been much more about the things you shouldn't do than those you should. This is the result of how the faith has characterized humanity ever since establishing the original sin doctrine. The message has been that despite being made in God's image humans are really a despicable bunch, far more naturally inclined to perform evil than good, so God justifiably casts them all into eternal hell. The only thing that can save them and turn them from evil to good is taking Jesus as their savior and following all the rules the faith has made to prevent them from living in the vile, disgusting ways they naturally would.

Of course, no one needs a reminder of all the horrifying evil that humanity has inflicted upon itself and all creation in its history. But the question we need to consider is are these evil tendencies natural or innate to the human species? Is evil due to a force, an impulse within us that is inextricably part of our genetic or psychological makeup? Is evil the "default" behavior of human beings and will naturally occur unless an opposing force is imposed upon it? Christianity has always stated the answers to these questions are yes, and only submission to the church can save humanity from this all-pervasive evil.

Thankfully there are other ways to consider this. First, the idea that the church is the only power that can overcome evil has been incontrovertibly refuted by the fact the church itself has been one of the greatest purveyors of evil since it began, and there shouldn't be a need to go into a lot of historical detail to substantiate that. Second, humanity has proven itself to be entirely capable of choosing and being a force for good in the world, and good has always been a much more prevalent emanation of humanity than evil. And most of the goodness in our world hasn't been the result of an allegiance with Jesus or from people beholden to the church's moral code. It's been from people just expressing the natural goodness they have as a part of their divine nature. God forbid what the world would be like if evil was really an innate power within humanity it was powerless to overcome.

If there is a characteristic that can be considered a natural behavior in human beings it is selfishness, and that has nothing to do with original sin forcing evil onto the entire human genome. It is the result of the seemingly inevitable creation of ego-identity in every person's psychological makeup, and it is very different from evil. The church has done humanity a tremendous disservice with the stain of evil it placed upon it, and it is up to us to see ourselves in a more positive light.

Does this mean that in MCU we have no need for a moral code or standards of behavior? No, it doesn't. But behind Christian Universalism is the belief that when we fully take on the spirit of our faith, we naturally become unwilling if not unable to violate those ethical standards the mainstream church has in place. When we feel the unconditional love God has for us, it doesn't, or at least shouldn't, occur to us that we can better ourselves or be happier somehow by harming or thinking badly of someone else in any way. The last five (or six, if we include honoring our parents, which I should remind my daughters of) of the Ten Commandments become superfluous.

In MCU, we look straight to the incarnate Christ for guidance on this (and every) matter of faith, and on this one he made his feelings very clear, as seen in Matt 22:37–40, when he issued what became known as the Great Commandments. When a scribe asked Jesus which is the greatest commandment, "He said to him 'You shall love the Lord your God with all your heart and with all your soul and with all your mind. This is the great and first commandment. And a second is like it: You shall love your neighbor as yourself. On these two commandments depend all the Law and the Prophets'" (ESV).

There's a lot to unpack here, but a good place to start is with the last sentence. What Jesus meant by it was that if we can follow these two commandments, we will also comply with all Ten Commandments and the entire moral code of Judaism as it was understood at the time, even the parts eventually included in the Hebrew Bible. But if you think that Jesus was being lenient by reducing all ethics and morality into two rules, consider the scope of what those two Great Commandments ask of us. There's more to them than you may think. Most significantly, when we follow them we not only comply with moral guidelines, but we also take some needed steps on the path to mystical realization.

The second one might be the easier of the two, but it's still a doozy. What must we do to truly love our neighbors as ourselves? It seems possible for those of us who can take their personal piety to an extreme, but is it really? At the very least, this commandment requires we cultivate our capacity for empathy and compassion to a greater degree, and we can honor it in part through the good works/love in action practices we just discussed. But the larger question still remains. Can people really care about the well-being of others as much as their own and be willing to sacrifice or bring detriment upon themselves to contribute to the health and happiness of others? Keep in mind "neighbor" in the Bible just means some random other person. It didn't mean a family member or even someone you knew or were fond of. It is at least a very tall order. Just being human seems to mean you have an innate self-interest that is greater than any other interest you can have. Would Jesus issue a commandment to us that is near impossible to keep?

Well, maybe that's the point. Surely Jesus knew that basic human nature would preclude us from fully obeying this commandment, but maybe he issued it anyway to make us understand that we must overcome our basic nature, and really, completely transform our sense of self, to make keeping it possible. It goes back to a topic we've discussed a lot already, which is how we pursue mystical experience and what Jesus expects of us to follow him to the kingdom of God. In this case, to "love your neighbor as yourself," your ego-identity has to be diminished so much in your consciousness you no longer think of yourself as an individual being with needs you must consider first. You don't conceive of yourself as a separate entity. You now live in oneness with all humanity, and your life is merged into the one great life each person is an expression of. You can "love your neighbor as yourself" because you no longer see your neighbor as separate from you. You are both a part of the same thing, the one divine reality.

If you are experiencing this state of consciousness, you are not just following the second of the Great Commandments. You have also taken a huge step on your mystical journey, which is why MCU holds these commandments in high regard and hopes people honor them to the best of their ability.

In the first of the Great Commandments, we see Jesus describing another requirement for Christ consciousness and the kingdom of God, even if it's not explicitly stated as such. But his words imploring us to love the Lord our God with all our mind, heart, and soul are reminiscent of other statements he made indicating how we must prioritize God over, and even to the exclusion of, anything else in our lives we hold dear or believe valuable. In the lilies of the field parable, he told us not to worry about our personal and physical needs and seek the kingdom of God above all else. Earlier we considered one of Jesus's most challenging statements when, in Luke 14:26, he said, "If anyone comes to me and does not hate father and mother, wife and children, brothers and sisters—yes, even their own life— such a person cannot be my disciple" (NIV).

The question we need to ask ourselves is what we must do to make this prioritization of God in our hearts, minds, and souls possible, and if you recall, the conclusion we came to in our previous discussion of Luke 14:26 was that we must undergo what Evelyn Underhill called the purgation/purification process, or the second stage of mysticism. So, that is why in MCU we have determined it must also be one of our essential spiritual practices.

Sorry, but No One Said This Would Be Easy

As much as MCU would like to offer a simple way of religious fulfillment, the evidence shows such a way doesn't exist. If we truly aspire to reach the pinnacle of spiritual and mystical experience, our primary objective in MCU, we must start by following the first of the Great Commandments. And to love God with all our mind, heart, and soul, as the commandment states, we must rid ourselves of everything in our lives that prevent us from doing so. These are the beliefs, values, interests, likes, and dislikes that our ego-identity has acquired from the world and constructed itself with. Whether you call it purgation/purification or renunciation (in MCU it's up to you!), you must subjugate or eliminate all the thoughts and behaviors from your conscious experience that distract you from your goal of God-realization.

The first of the Great Commandments is very similar to the first of the Ten Commandments in a significant way. Both are violated when something besides God is of supreme importance and the top priority in a person's life. "You shall have no other gods before me" doesn't mean deities from other religions as it is often thought. Anything that one's ego-identity has placed first and foremost in consciousness can be considered that person's god. It can be any one of a number of things, such as romantic or sexual interest, personal finances, professional or career life, political affiliation, or even a favorite sports team. If these or other things occupy your mind to the extent your desire for God-realization becomes secondary, these commandments are not being followed as they should.

Basically, we must take an inventory of everything we've always considered important in our lives and assess how much they still mean to us. What people often discover is the things, opinions, beliefs, and enjoyments they've derived from the world over the course of their lives no longer interest or provide them with pleasure, purpose, or satisfaction. Then, after evaluating themselves further, they have a more profound realization. They realize there isn't anything they can experience in their ego-controlled consciousness that is remotely close to the contentment and bliss awaiting them in spiritual fulfillment, and that's why they're aspiring mystics in the first place. They must transform themselves from self-centered beings to God or soul-centered beings if they are to get the satisfaction from life they seek. These are the people who become laser-focused on their spirituality and discontinue all other interests, enjoyments, and in some cases, relationships, that may interfere with their divine purpose.

What would that look like? We considered some possibilities earlier, but certainly some people in this group would eliminate their media exposure, remove every function from their phones that's not for making calls, and discontinue hobbies or other outside interests. Basically, anything that isn't necessitated in their immediate experience of life, meaning in most cases what a person does to support themselves financially and maintain loving relationships in their home, will be considered nonessential and discarded, so that the rest of their time can be devoted to their spiritual quest.

And yes, there will be some aspirants who will take it even further than that, meaning they will reach the conclusion they must remove themselves from greater society and commit to a cloistered or solitary life. This is a monumental decision for anyone to make and those who do should be respected for their courage and convictions.

What we in MCU expect however is that the large majority of people who go through the purgation/purification process won't reach those same conclusions, even if they have a strong desire to attain mystical realization and believe it is the divinely ordained purpose of their lives. Their ego-identity attachments are still too strong and meaningful to them, so, they will attempt to compartmentalize the spiritual and worldly aspects of their lives to the best of their ability and try to fulfill their potential in both realms. This is understandable and absolutely OK. Most people do not experience their lives, even under the control of their egos, as entirely negative, and thank God for that. Our souls are all in different stages of their eternal journeys and it's to be expected that those who aren't as spiritually evolved wouldn't feel as driven to pursue spiritual fulfillment as those farther along the cosmic highway. Isn't this something we see all the time? We've all known people who from childhood on have seemed to be seekers, dreamers, or born contemplatives (like your humble writer, for example). Most others have much more practical temperaments and feel very much at home in the world.

The bottom line here is, regardless of the degree of religious motivation a person may feel, we believe that MCU offers a way for them to maximize their spiritual well-being and understanding. As for me, I could really relate to someone who aspires to be the next great Christian mystic but hopes that doesn't mean he wouldn't care if his team is in the World Series. We would absolutely get along great.

Pastor Peter's First Christian Universalist Church, Mystical

My hope is this following segment attracts the attention of my brethren in Christian Universalist ministry or any clergy that is so inclined. If you are intrigued by what you have read so far and wonder how MCU would be ministered in a parish setting, some thoughts on that will be shared here. For readers who may be inclined to attend or become members of a hypothetical MCU church, some light on what that may be like will be shed here as well.

The Christian Universalist Church in America has existed in some way since John Murray presided over the first CU church service in Good Luck (now Lacey Township), New Jersey, on September 30, 1770.[7] Murray went on to found the first Universalist church in Gloucester, Massachusetts, in 1774,[8] and later helped create our first denomination, the Universalist Church of America (UCA), in 1793.[9] The UCA was absorbed into the Unitarian Universalist Association in 1961, and the resulting dissatisfaction with that among Universalists factored into the creation of the Christian Universalist Association in 2007.

This brief CU history lesson is only to point out that for most of the past 250 years there has been, in some form or name, churches operating and holding Sunday services that have at least a historic connection to CU. And the people who attended these church services had an experience very much like they could have had at any Reformed Christian church from the 1770s to today.

The same would be true in MCU. The MCU church service, as it is now being envisioned (and this is very much a work in progress), will differ in just very minor ways from any CU or mainline Protestant service that's been held anytime this century. It will have all the liturgical elements people are accustomed to, such as calls to worship, hymns, invocations,

7. Howe, *Larger*, 2.

8. Howe, *Larger*, 6.

9. Howe, *Larger*, 1.

Bible readings and lessons, pastoral prayers, sermons, benedictions, etc., etc. We'll honor all the traditional sacraments, including baptism and communion. The only notable addition would be a guided meditation, in which people will be led to the mindful space in their consciousness where they exist in peace and oneness with God. Other than that, it's pretty much business as usual.

The biggest difference in MCU Sunday services will be how they are experienced holistically and thematically. Those longtime enemies of God and humanity, eternal hell, original sin, and vicarious atonement, will be consistently and powerfully rejected and discredited. There will be a greater orientation toward Group One spirituality and a more metaphysical exegesis of Scripture. People will be taught to consider how certain passages can be interpreted as describing conscious states, not actual events. Sermons would also follow this thematic pattern, meaning a much greater focus on universal salvation and the kingdom of God being a state of consciousness, not a place or location.

Of course, as any parish priest or minister will tell you, church is a seven-day-a-week thing and Sundays, while important, are just a small part of parish ministry and the life of a church. In MCU churches there would ideally be a midweek meditation service, as well as classes and workshops on mindfulness meditation. If there is a meditation center or community close to your MCU church, it would be fabulous to offer parishioners periodic weekend retreats there. If you're near a state park or nature reserve of some kind, perhaps day trips could be arranged so that nature contemplation can be explored and experienced.

However, just as important as the orientation to Group One spirituality, MCU churches need to have a robust love in action component that people can be strongly encouraged to participate in. This would take the form of establishing relationships with local charities, such as food banks or care for the homeless, and also affiliating with global projects that address greater issues like poverty and climate change. MCU churches will emphasize the importance of being a source of goodness in the world and provide the opportunities to perform this good on a larger scale.

Finally, the most distinctive element of the MCU church will be how it provides guidance on and assists people with the practice of purgation/purification. MCU cannot teach that this is an essential part of our spiritual practice unless we explain why it is so vital and offer people the tools and capabilities to undertake this practice themselves.

Basically, the MCU church will provide an institution and community in which people who are attracted to "the new way of Christian faith" we described MCU as being, can find the fellowship, education, and support to make practicing MCU a more fulfilling experience.

As Wordsworth Said, "The Child is Father to the Man"

"I Remember, I Remember" by Thomas Hood

I remember, I remember,
The house where I was born,
The little window where the sun
Came peeping in at morn;
He never came a wink too soon,
Nor brought too long a day,
But now, I often wish the night
Had borne my breath away!
I remember, I remember,
The roses, red and white,
The vi'lets, and the lily-cups,
Those flowers made of light!
The lilacs where the robin built,
And where my brother set
The laburnum on his birthday,
The tree is living yet!

I remember, I remember,
Where I was used to swing,
And thought the air must rush as fresh
To swallows on the wing;
My spirit flew in feathers then,
That is so heavy now,
And summer pools could hardly cool
The fever on my brow!

I remember, I remember,
The fir trees dark and high;
I used to think their slender tops
Were close against the sky:
It was a childish ignorance,
But now 'tis little joy

To know I'm farther off from heav'n
Than when I was a boy.[10]

"Then people brought little children to Jesus for him to place his hands on them and pray for them. But the disciples rebuked them. Jesus said, 'Let the little children come to me, and do not hinder them, for the kingdom of heaven belongs to such as these'" (Matt 19:13–14 NIV).

"And He called a child to Himself and set him before them, and said, 'Truly I say to you, unless you are converted and become like children, you will not enter the kingdom of heaven. Whoever then humbles himself as this child, he is the greatest in the kingdom of heaven'" (Matt 18:2–4 NASB).

When we started to think about ministry to children in our MCU church, we realized there is more to childhood spirituality than we thought. What we learned, as the two passages above from Matthew suggest, is that the consciousness of childhood may be more like kingdom of God or Christ consciousness than what most adults will experience, so we really have as much to learn from our children as we have to teach them.

As the poem "I Remember, I Remember" conveys, there is a timeless appeal to the childhood mind. Virtually every adult at some point feels a longing for their childhood. Who among us hasn't wished they could go back in time and relive their six-, seven-, or eight-year-old consciousness again? Yet it's not clear what we are longing for, or what we have lost and hope to regain. Is the conscious state we vaguely recall a mystical one, even if we can't quite grasp it? People most commonly believe it is the quality of innocence they recall and that is what Jesus is referring to as well. There is something pure and magical about the childhood mind that disappears when we reach puberty and reproductive maturity, and innocence is certainly some of what we lose. But there remains a feeling there is more to it than that. What Jesus implies in Matthew is that children have a stronger conscious connection to the kingdom of God than adults do. If that's the conscious state we've lost, it's understandable why many of us feel an innate need to recapture it and why Jesus is telling us we need to do so.

But what is it about the conscious awareness of children that brings them closer to God-realization and why does it move further away as we age? One theory is that because children are the most recent arrivals from the spiritual realm and haven't been tainted by life on Earth yet, they are naturally closer to the kingdom of God and are born with a greater awareness of and connection to the Divine. Okay. I don't have a problem with

10. Hood, "I Remember."

that, and once you accept the existence of the spiritual realm it makes as much sense as anything else. But more obviously, we can see that children are more fully immersed in the world. They see themselves as part of the all. It's as if they are born with the enchanted worldview adults need to recreate in themselves. As the child in "I Remember, I Remember" rides the swing, gazes at flowers, and watches the sunrise, he is enthralled by the magic and aliveness of it all. He, like all children, sees reality with greater clarity than adults do. Children don't have the psychic veil or shadow that casts a pall over the adult experience of life.

It may be helpful, when we ponder what this vital quality of the childhood mind is, to refer back to our earlier discussion of ego-identity development. Childhood consciousness is not wrapped up in self-identity yet. They haven't had the thirty- or forty-odd years of life that our egos use to create the false sense of identity that isolates us, disenchants us, and instills an illusion of separateness and detachment from the world. Children are blissfully free from those psychic confines.

So, if it is ego-identity that dispels the child consciousness Jesus likened to the kingdom of God, how can we recapture it? How do we lift the veil and "become like children" again? In MCU, we believe we can do this by engaging in all the practices we've already discussed. When we meditate on the Christ within, worshipfully contemplate nature, and release as many ego attachments as we can, we will find ourselves in a pristine, childlike conscious state in which the divine nature of our souls and creation become more apparent. In a sense, this is what we can consider being "born again." Our lives and minds are transformed and revitalized, and it is much like starting life anew and being a child once more.

What does this mean for the religious education of children in MCU? Unfortunately, not much, at least at this time. There's only so much any local church can offer for childhood religious formation. We certainly envision Sunday children's lessons, using teaching materials that conform to CU beliefs and values. Our children's program should also include introducing and instructing them in the meditative arts.

There is, however, another concept floating around the cranium. To say it's embryonic is probably overstating it. If some parts of this book weren't completely baked, this hasn't even gone in the oven yet, so bear with me. What I'm envisioning is somehow finding a way to work with children so they can retain all that is great about childhood consciousness as long into their lives as possible. I don't have a clue about how it would work. It would involve working with child psychologists just to see if it's feasible or possible, but if it is, how cool would that be?

There are psychologists now who work with people in the psychedelic community to help them "integrate" whatever insights or wisdom they feel their experiences afforded them, so they can retain them in their everyday lives. Would something like that help children hold onto the spiritual vision and enchanted perspective with which they view the world? If it is these things that Jesus said gives children access to the kingdom of God, isn't it in the best interests of all humanity if those gifts could become lifelong and not fade so quickly? Wouldn't we then be able to hasten the day when our Savior, Christ consciousness, lifts humanity up to its ultimate destiny of unity and oneness with our Creator and Divine Source of All Being?

It's at least fun to think about, wouldn't you say?

Epilogue

So Where Are We Now?

I CAN SEE IT now. A Sunday (let's make it Palm Sunday) version of the New York Times or Washington Post. The year is 2060. The lead story of the day, written especially for the week before Easter, starts like this. *As we embark on a new decade and review the religious tenor of our nation as Holy Week begins, the astounding rise of Christian Universalism towers over everything else. CU is now the largest Christian denomination in the country and has completely reshaped how Christians in America experience their faith. In fact, no other development in the last thirty to forty years has unified the country as much as the rise of CU has. The issues that once polarized America seem to have withered away, thanks to CU's healing effects. Religious vs. secular, science vs. religion, even cultural liberal vs. cultural conservative, all the old conflicts that once seemed to hopelessly divide us now barely raise a ripple on the national landscape. How has this even been possible? Social scientists are almost unanimous in their belief that once people in large numbers began to understand God as the unconditionally loving Source and Substance of All Being, and that eternal life and divine love graces all of humanity, the divisions promoted by sectarian religious leaders were finally recognized for their absurdity and destructiveness.*

The rise of Christian Universalism can be traced all the way back to the early twenties, when CU minister and author Peter Stilla introduced a mystical branch of the faith in a new book that became a nationwide bestseller. Mystical Christian Universalism (MCU) seemed to excite and motivate the young adults of that generation who previously would have rejected Christianity and turn to atheism or agnosticism. They realized that through MCU they could be Christian and have rich and rewarding spiritual lives, because they didn't have to tie their spirituality to a God they were told is sadistic and genocidal and was ridiculed by the world of science.

Actually, my ego-identity made me write at least the first sentence of that last paragraph. But the rest of it is truly up to us. We can make this vision manifest in reality if we hold it in our hearts and project it into our world each day. The key is never forgetting that God and truth are on our side, and it is inevitable that someday this truth will emerge ascendent and triumphant in the collective heart of humanity. All of creation is on an inexorable path to deliverance and perfection in Christ, and our job is to expedite the process by spreading this message as far and wide as we can.

Of course, it would be wrong to say the road ahead will be smooth and simple. When we look at our current cultural and religious environment, we see a lot of obstacles. It's difficult to see how humanity and creation can be on an onward and upward trajectory. Where is the unity and harmony amongst us that would be evidence of that, and we will need to carry us forward? Can we really be heading in the positive direction described in our news story when the forces of conflict and division are as insidious and dangerous as they now seem to be?

As this is being written there is a group of supposed Christians plotting a fascist takeover of our government, hoping to replace democracy with some type of authoritarian theocracy. The people at the forefront of this movement call themselves Christian nationalists, even though they are neither patriots nor truly Christian, at least in any genuine, authentic way that wouldn't horrify Jesus. In fact, it's not a stretch to say that it is more of a Caucasian nationalist movement disguising itself by using the word "Christian." Making it especially frustrating is this movement is seen by many people in this country as representative of all Christianity. So, it seems as if those of us on the right side of Christ have to battle on two fronts. First, we must overcome the considerable power with which the race-based wing of the Church imposes itself on the rest of us. Then we have to convince the vast majority of our citizenry, which values democracy and the separation of church and state, that we are Christians who are on their side and want the same things they do.

Or do we? Yes, these are challenging times, but getting caught up in conflict and all we seemingly have to overcome will not help our cause. As Christian Universalists, we just need to stay true to ourselves. For one thing, we are representing the perspective of enlightened, mystical consciousness, and in that conscious state it isn't possible to see other human beings as enemies or opponents in any way, even when that is how they are seeing us. Of course, we aren't immune to provocation and could feel our egos tempting us to respond to hate and aggression in the same way. But what would that do but reveal we are in the same deplorable spiritual condition as those who want to defeat us? If there was ever a time when Christian Universalists need to pay heed to Matt 5:39, "but I tell you, do not resist an evil person. If anyone slaps you on the right cheek, turn to them the other cheek also" (NIV), it is in the task before us of promoting and bearing witness to the truth in the face of evil, blasphemy, and falsehood.

As always, we can see in the example of Jesus the way we need to follow. Even in the face of brutal persecution that resulted in his crucifixion, Jesus stayed steadfast on the path of nonresistance, and ultimately, it was the truth, the Christ, that emerged triumphant. So too it will for us and all humanity. The truth always emerges eventually, even if in our current moment it is hard to envision and seems a long way off. Rest assured that victory is already ours and its arrival is inevitable. In the meantime, all we need to do is stay nonresistant to those who would oppose us, live our faith, speak our truth as we know it, and pursue Christ consciousness as best we can. We can't possibly fail.

A couple of things in our 2060 Palm Sunday news feature may have gone under the radar some, so let's take a closer look at them. First will be the part that describes MCU bridging our seemingly intractable cultural divides. Science or secularism vs. religion, conservative vs. liberal? Really? How is that possible?

It may surprise some of you to hear that the once canyon-like divide between science and religion has softened a lot already, starting in the latter half of the twentieth century. The discovery of quantum mechanics was an earthquake under the ground of scientific determinism. Suddenly, scientists who have long insisted that the physical composition of the universe is all there was to existence and reality were forced to question their previously unshakable beliefs. Especially in the field of physics, there has been a greater willingness to concede there is a mysterious gap in what the scientific method is able to discover about reality at the atomic and subatomic levels.

What has the potential of closing that gap a lot more if not completely is the principle of panentheism, especially in how it is proposed in process philosophy. As it turns out, science's main objection to the concept of divine activity in reality is more based on understanding it as a supernatural incursion from a realm that somehow exists outside the physical universe. Bringing the divine and natural together in the way that panentheism and process philosophy so cogently does has taken a lot of wind from the sails of spiritual existence deniers. In other words, the scientific community is a lot more comfortable with Divinity as we understand it in Mystical Christian Universalism than they are with the flowing-robe God that throws lightning bolts from some great beyond, especially coming as it often does from people who reject and deny science at every opportunity. So, I think it's fair to say that as MCU grows and the panentheistic concept of Divinity and reality grows along with it, the potential is there to find more common ground between the religious and scientific perspectives.

Cultural liberals and cultural conservatives holding hands and singing kumbaya? OK, maybe I'm going off the deep end with this one, but maybe not. First, the word "cultural" is used here to distinguish these groups from their political brethren, as what follows isn't related to differing views on proper governance, even as our political parties pander to both sides of the cultural divide. But if there is a word that can be used almost interchangeably with "cultural," especially for conservatives, it is "religious." If there is one thing that cultural conservatism is rooted in more than anything else, it is religious conservatism. It's even reasonable to believe that without religious conservatism, very little of the cultural conservative movement would continue to exist, besides that which is undeniably based on xenophobia and racial animus.

Let's consider one of the issues cultural conservatives seem to consider most important, and which no doubt derives from their religious perspective. This is their stance on stigmatizing the LGBTQ community and seeking the legal means to discriminate against them, which they describe as an expression of "religious freedom" and usually justify with just a single verse from Leviticus. This seems to be part of a broader pattern in which any variation of sexual gender, activity, or orientation outside heterosexual marriage is to be demonized, because of the perception that is what the God of the Christian Bible wants.

The larger point is because cultural conservatives are so closely tied with right-wing, sectarian Christianity, it colors their entire worldview and perspective on reality. Life is a zero-sum game for them and their religious beliefs demand that they distinguish themselves as the game's winners, and everyone who doesn't belong to their team (LGBTQ, Jews, infidels, etc.) must be considered opponents they must either convert or defeat. It is what

God demands of them in exchange for being victorious in God's game of life. And why wouldn't they believe this, considering they conceive of God as willing to mete out eternal, ultimate punishment to all the game's losers who don't submit to their tortured belief system. There isn't even a willingness to believe that cultural liberals could also be people of faith and that their beliefs and values could be religiously motivated. If you are not in agreement with them on any cultural issue it's because you're an atheist, anti-God, or anti-Christian.

Now, considering this situation has just been depicted in a way that makes the reconciliation of science and religion look like it took place in Golden Gate Park during the Summer of Love, it's reasonable to wonder how could Christian Universalism possibly address it? Yes, it does seem a lot to ask. But the vision is that as CU continues to grow and increases its visibility, people from more conservative Christian churches, especially those in what M. Scott Peck called the skeptic/individual stage of spiritual growth, can start to be won over. These are the people that have a lot of questions and doubts about the conservative church and are looking for answers and a way of exploring their spirituality further, and lo and behold, there CU will be. And as this movement keeps growing, a tipping point or a point of critical mass will be reached, and the conservative church just may be willing to concede there is a legitimate Christian counterpoint to their cultural arguments. The absolutism of their viewpoints may fade just enough to allow for the relationship between cultural/religious conservatives and liberals to become more conciliatory and less adversarial.

But of much greater significance. . .

However, when we consider the future of CU/MCU and the potential it has to impact our larger cultural and religious milieu, without first thinking about how it can transform the lives of the millions of people who feel spiritually lost, confused, and alone, we are putting the proverbial cart before the proverbial horse. If CU/MCU can really come to the spiritual rescue of those who are searching for something to feed their souls and enlighten their minds, then all the rosy scenarios we've discussed will take care of themselves. They will undoubtedly come to pass.

This point comes into greater focus for me when I consider the path my own life has taken, especially as a part of the generation I grew up in. I'm a baby boomer, and like so many others of that era, I witnessed the youth of my generation driven away from faith and spirituality by forces greater than they could resist. It wasn't the sexual revolution that turned us away, nor the rise of recreational drug use, or even the "immoral" influence of rock music, even though the conservative church pointed its finger of blame at all those things. The truth is nothing from that generation, or really all those before and since, has produced more atheism, agnosticism, or irreligion than the conservative church itself.

Modern, decently educated people from the mid-twentieth century on instinctively know church doctrine on God and humanity is egregiously false and corrupt, unless they are those poor unfortunates who have been brutally indoctrinated into the church from a young age. What they also instinctively know or at least feel is that what is lacking in their lives isn't religious faith but religious *experience*. This is as true now as it was tens or hundreds of thousands of years ago, before there was such a thing as a religion to belong to. This is the story of humanity and always will be. It is the conscious realization or ascertainment of God, also known as the mystical experience, that is the only thing that can fulfill the spiritual longing we are all born with. And to have that fulfillment is the only thing we are all born for.

Bibliography

"Anatta." New World Encyclopedia, last updated Mar 19, 2016. https://www.newworld encyclopedia.org/p/index.php?title=Anatta&oldid=994683.

Bridgeman, Jacqueline Hazard, ed. *Huxley and God: Essays*. San Francisco: Harper SanFrancisco, 1992.

Bucke, Richard Maurice. *Cosmic Consciousness*. New York: E. P. Dutton, 1901. http://djm. cc/library/Cosmic_Consciousness_edited02.pdf.

Coxhead, Nona. *The Relevance of Bliss*. New York: St. Martin's, 1985.

Dass, Ram. *Be Here Now*. San Anselmo, CA: Hanuman Foundation, 1971.

"Emanationism." New World Encyclopedia, last updated Sep 12, 2017. https://www. newworldencyclopedia.org/p/index.php?title=Emanationism&oldid=1006726.

"Eschatology." New World Encyclopedia, last updated Feb 20, 2022. https://www. newworldencyclopedia.org/p/index.php?title=Eschatology&oldid=1065165.

Fox, Matthew, ed. *Breakthrough: Meister Eckhart's Creation Spirituality in New Translation*. Garden City, NY: Doubleday, 1980.

Fristad, Kalen. *Destined for Salvation: God's Promise to Save Everyone*. Kearney, NE: Morris, 2003.

Goldsmith, Joel S. *A Parenthesis in Eternity: Living the Mystical Life*. New York: Harper and Row, 1963.

Griffin, David Ray. *Reenchantment without Supernaturalism: A Process Philosophy of Religion*. Ithica, NY: Cornell University Press, 2001.

Grim, John, and Mary Evelyn Tucker. "Biography of Teilhard de Chardin." American Teilhard Association, n.d. https://teilharddechardin.org/teilhard-de-chardin/ biography-of-teilhard-de-chardin/.

Hanson, J. W. *Universalism: The Prevailing Doctrine of the Christian Church During Its First Five Hundred Years*. Boston: Universalist, 1899. https://archive.org/details/ universalismpreoohansgoog/page/n18/mode/2up.

Hood, Thomas. "I Remember, I Remember." Poetry Foundation, n.d. https://www. poetryfoundation.org/poems/44387/i-remember-i-remember.

Howe, Charles A. *The Larger Faith: A Short History of Christian Universalism*. Boston: Skinner House, 1993.

James, William. *The Varieties of Religious Experience*. New York: Modern Library, 1936.

"Jesus Prayer." Encyclopedia Britannica, last updated Aug 24, 2017. https://www.britannica .com/topic/Jesus-prayer.

Johnson, Raynor C. *Watcher on the Hills*. New York: Harper and Brothers, 1959.

Johnston, William, ed. *The Cloud of Unknowing and the Book of Privy Counseling*. New York: Doubleday Image, 1973.

Koestler, Arthur. *The Invisible Writing*. New York: Macmillan, 1954.

"Letter of James." Encyclopedia Britannica, last updated Aug 20, 2020. https://www. britannica.com/topic/Letter-of-James.

Lyons, J.A. *The Cosmic Christ in Origen and Teilhard de Chardin: A Comparative Study*. Oxford: Oxford University Press, 1982.

Maharshi, Ramana. "Death Experience." Sri Ramanasramam, Jan 20, 2013. https://www. sriramanamaharshi.org/ramana-maharshi/death-experience/.

———. "Instructions." Sri Ramanasramam, n.d. https://www.sriramanamaharshi.org/ teachings/instructions/.

———. *Talks With Sri Ramana Maharshi: Extract Version*. Tamil Nadu, India: Sri Ramanasramam Tiruvannamalai, 2000. https://www.sriramanamaharshi.org/wp-content/uploads/2012/12/Talks_Exract.pdf.

———. "Who Am I?" Sri Ramanasramam, Jun 30, 1982. https://www.sriramanamaharshi. org/wp-content/uploads/2012/12/who_am_I.pdf.

Manneh, Elizabeth. "Lectio Divina: A Beginner's Guide." Busted Halo, Mar 1, 2023. https://bustedhalo.com/ministry-resources/lectio-divina-beginners-guide.

McLean, Sarah. *Soul-Centered: Transform Your Life in 8 Weeks with Meditation*. Carlsbad, CA: Hay House, 2012.

"Mesopotamian Religion." New World Encyclopedia, n.d. https://www.newworld encyclopedia.org/p/index.php?title=Mesopotamian_Religion&oldid=822991.

Milos, Joy. "Underhill's Mysticism: A Centenary Review." The Evelyn Underhill Association, Nov 8, 2011. http://evelynunderhill.org/underhills-mysticism-a-centenary-review-by-joy-milos/.

"Mystical Experience of Irina Starr." Institute for Mystical Experience Research and Education, n.d. https://imere.org/third-party-story/mystical-experience-irina-starr/.

"Mystical Experience of Jane Goodall, Ph.D." Institute for Mystical Experience Research and Education, n.d. https://imere.org/third-party-story/mystical-experience-jane-goodall-phd/.

"Mystical Experience of Madame Guyon." Institute for Mystical Experience Research and Education, n.d. https://imere.org/third-party-story/mystical-experience-madam-guyon/.

Osborn, Arthur W. *The Expansion of Awareness*. Wheaton, IL: Theosophical, 1967.

"Our Beliefs." Christian Universalist Association, n.d. https://christianuniversalist.org/ beliefs/.

"Panentheism." New World Encyclopedia, last updated Mar 11, 2023. https://www. newworldencyclopedia.org/entry/Panentheism.

Peck, M. Scott. *Further Along the Road Less Traveled*. New York: Simon and Schuster, 1993.

Pollan, Michael. *How to Change Your Mind*. New York: Penguin, 2018.

Roberts, Bernadette. *The Experience of No-Self*. Sunspot, NM: Iroquois House, 1982.

Rohr, Richard. *The Universal Christ*. New York: Convergent, 2019.

Sadat, Anwar. *In Search of Identity*. New York: Harper and Row, 1977.

"Sanskrit Literature." New World Encyclopedia, last updated Dec 23, 2022. https://www. newworldencyclopedia.org/p/index.php?title=Sanskrit_literature&oldid=1092646.

Stahl, Louann. *A Most Surprising Song: Exploring the Mystical Experience.* Unity Village, MO: Unity, 1992.

Suso, Henry. *The Life of Blessed Henry Suso.* Translated by Thomas Francis Knox. London: Burns, Lambert, and Oates, 1865. https://ia902607.us.archive.org/32/items/lifeof blessedhenooseus/lifeofblessedhenooseus.pdf.

Teilhard de Chardin, Pierre. *The Phenomenon of Man.* New York: Harper and Row, 1965.

Tolle, Eckhart. *The Power of Now: A Guide to Spiritual Enlightenment.* Vancouver, BC: Namaste, 1999.

Underhill, Evelyn. *Mysticism: A Study in the Nature and Development of Spiritual Consciousness.* New York: E. P. Dutton, 1912. https://ia600207.us.archive.org/16/ items/mysticismstudyinooundeuoft/mysticismstudyin00undeuoft.pdf.

Wilber, Ken, ed. *Quantum Questions: Mystical Writings of the World's Great Physicists..* Boston: Shambhala, 2001.

Younghusband, Sir Francis. *Heart of Nature.* London: John Murray, 1921. https://archive. org/details/dli.pahar.2148/page/168/mode/2up.